THE ART OF STEALING

I0424838

STRATEGIC SECURITY SOLUTIONS

MAJOR CHARLES READ

ISBN: 9781453746806

Publisher Information

ACCLAIM FOR WORKS BY MAJOR CHARLES READ, USAF

- ***MAXIMUM SECURITY...Defusing the Threat***
- ***Principles of Security Consulting***

"Charlie Read has written the best study of security consulting on the full range of issues that a security consultant could encounter..." -Sam J. Ofshinsky, Safety and Security executive with GE/NBC and CBS, Security Consultant to Fortune 500 firms and the US Government, and former FBI Contracting Agent

"Charlie Read, whose law enforcement and private sector security experience is exceptionally broad, now presents another "must have" addition to any law enforcement or security professional's library..." –Michael J. Hawley, Esquire

"In these uncertain times, security consultants and their customers can be sure of one thing; you need this book!' '...don't cut corners with safety – security starts right here! –William J. Gorta, Former Associate Editor, NY Post; Fulbright Research Fellow; Captain (retired) NYPD; Member of the original COMPSTAT team..."

"Comprehensive and well presented. We adopted Charlie's book, *Principles of Security Consulting*, as the text for the award of the Certified Security Consultant designation. Don't even think of entering the Security business unless you read this book." –Joseph Alercia, II, JD; Founder & CEO, Lion Investigation Academy; President, American Detective Agency

"Well presented, comprehensive, and most informative... 'Anyone serious about a professional Security or Public Safety career should read this book." –Robert Abraham, Chief of Police (retired), Sea Gate, NY; Inspector (retired) NYPD; Former Professor of Criminal Justice, John Jay College..."

"...An excellent book dealing with the basics of security consulting. Drawn upon his extensive experience in the security business, Charles Read has set out everything you need to know but were afraid to ask because you should have known it already. Well written and easy to read, this book will be an essential reference for both students and well-seasoned practitioners."
–Edward F. Cunningham, Esquire, Vice President, Global Consulting, Brinks, Inc. and former FBI Special Agent

MAJOR CHARLES READ, USAF

Charles Read is the author of *MAXIMUM SECURITY...Defusing the Threat* and *PRINCIPLES OF SECURITY CONSULTING*, his troubleshooting and problem-solving services have been sought by executives, Fortune companies, law offices, accounting firms, and police departments since 1993.

Mr. Read provides strategic solutions for a select clientele. He specializes in adverse incident response and interim leadership engagements and provides executives with the tools, information, and methodologies needed to detect, deter, and resolve problems and make informed decisions. He and his partnered associates comprise a sophisticated assemblage of security specialists, investigators, intelligence experts, and special operatives from law enforcement agencies, international security consulting firms, and the military Special Operations community.

CONTACT

DUE TO THE SENSITIVE NATURE OF CLIENT NEEDS, MEETINGS ARE BY APPOINTMENT ONLY:

CALICO SCRIBE
PO BOX 8066
DUCK, NC 27949
(www) calicoscribe.com

DEDICATION

Many victims of crime cannot properly defend themselves - this book is dedicated to the courageous men and women who are committed to protecting the people, places and things who find themselves victims of those who choose crime and hate over respect and love for their fellow man – blue lives matter!

"The liberties of our country, the freedom of our civil constitution, are worth defending against all hazards: And it is our duty to defend them against all attacks." – Samuel Adams

FOREWORD

In his books, *PRINCIPLES OF SECURITY CONSULTING* and *MAXIMUM SECURITY ...Defusing the Threat...,* we quickly learn that security in any form is, as Charlie Read says, "as much a perception as it is a reality" and begins with acceptance by the individual... His style is designed to have you think and act unconventionally regarding security matters.

As you read this work, keep in mind that Major Read is a security professional with significant experience in developing and managing security programs from an unconventional point of view, both as a special operations officer in the military and now as a civilian consultant. His significant operational career experience and unconventional approach to security is coupled with a down-to-earth training and writing style that presents a fantastic, readable, and relevant text on what it takes to become not just a good security consultant, but a great security consultant. After all, security is a state of mind.

-Richard F. Forno, PhD, author of *The Art of Information Warfare, Incident Response,* and *Weapons of Mass Delusion.* Doctor Forno is a Senior Lecturer at UMBC and a former Senior Security Analyst for the U.S. House of Representatives.

TABLE OF CONTENTS

AUTHOR'S MESSAGE

This work is designed to help you help others!

Crime-based threats continue to be a major and growing problem in both their social implications and in their difficulty to prevent and have been exacerbated by hate.

Numerous studies report that crimes are often perpetrated by persons who don't know their victims and that victims are often selected based on how they look, or how they or their security posture are perceived.

The criminal is more likely to strike a soft target of opportunity. Potential crime victims must change how their security posture might be perceived by others by HARDENING THE TARGET and we, as a society and those in representative organizations, must take positive measures to protect those who fall victim to crime and protect those who can't protect themselves.

"The best way to find yourself is to lose yourself in the service of others." – Gandhi

AUTHOR'S DISCLAIMER: *THE ART OF STEALING* is a comparable and companion work to *END THE HATE,* therefore a good deal of the information in these works is much the same and the works are essentially interchangeable.

INTRODUCTION

COMBATTING SECURITY THREATS

Fueled by the rapid response and extensive exposure in the news, crimes have become more visible and prevalent in recent years - not a day goes by that we don't hear of a horrific crime being perpetrated somewhere. Driven by alarming crime statistics and staggering losses, organizations of all kinds have both a need and an obligation to protect their personnel and resources – targets of crime-based threats are among the most vulnerable and they must place an emphasis on establishing effective security strategies.

PLANNING FOR SECURITY: No single book is going to provide all the information needed to combat crime-based threats, therefore the reader is directed to the professional services, publications, and references contained herein, often offered free of charge, to gather the latest information and to obtain assistance in developing plans, programs, protocols, and strategies that when properly applied, will detect and deter crime and criminality and instill a sense of safety and security in and among their organizations and communities. These materials are provided by several government agencies as well as the several outstanding professional security organizations.

"Safety is something that happens between your ears, not something you hold in your hands." -Jeff Cooper

PROLOGUE

CRIME has far reaching and often devastating effects on the community at large and especially upon those in the community who share the same or like characteristics of the victims. This secondary victimization creates similar experiences of fear and vulnerability and creates separate yet equally important and unique challenges to provide security and restore a sense of safety. When victims of crimes are selected based on personal characteristics such as their actual or perceived weaknesses, ethnicity, disability, national origin, race, religion, or sexual orientation, all within that and the extended community are impacted and instilled with the fear of becoming a victim of violence and that fear, that terror, can be nearly as debilitating as suffering through the actual crime. Violent crimes frequently have broadly disruptive social effects and often lead to greater distrust of law enforcement and additional friction between racial or religious communities.

Crime provokes tensions which often triggers widespread conflict within communities. Serious crimes put everyone at-risk of domestic, social, and economic consequences. The actual financial costs attributed to crimes are staggering but the costs in terms of human suffering are immeasurable. Polls taken each year indicate that the fear of crime is a growing problem. In recent years crimes against persons and property have instilled in many a constant fear of being victimized on the street, at work, in their houses of worship, and even in their homes.

Without question, the crime-rate coupled with graphic depictions of violent crime by the news media has contributed to a reduction of a feeling of safety, security, and serenity and has increased the need for enhanced security.

"I destroy my enemies when I make them my friends" – Abraham Lincoln

STRATEGIES

This work provides the reader with the tools, technologies, techniques, methodologies, and resources necessary to HARDEN THE TARGET by developing affordable and effective protective protocols for those entrusted with caring for others; there is no more noble cause than to Protect and Serve, Winston Churchill said: *"We make a living by what we get, we make a life by what we give."*

Having identified the culprit, let us direct our attention to Combatting Crime-Based Security Threats:

Most law enforcement agencies don't have the means to provide full coverage security service for private individuals or organizations. Americans are confronted with a constant fear of crime and they are seeking services beyond the capacity of the nation's over-committed and understaffed public law enforcement agencies. In most major cities, private security, including in-house resources, plays a significant role in maintaining order and providing safety and security.

The leaders and administrators of all organizations have an obligation to their members and the community at-large to develop, implement, and enforce effective safety and security programs. This work takes the reader through the three-step process of developing an effective security and safety posture: assessment, planning, and implementation, the process proceeds step-by-step beginning with the development of basic plans, the conduct of vulnerability assessments, the assembly of safety and security committees, and ultimately the formal program.

The arbitrary manner in which victims are frequently targeted is profoundly unsettling and increases the difficulty of pro-actively identifying perpetrators. The reader is encouraged to cultivate a culture of observance and attention to detail. In the end, observation is the first and best defense and when combined with accurate assessment, thorough planning and enforced implementation, an overall sense of safety and security is established.

Whatever the situation, most administrators would agree that their number one goal is to provide a safe, peaceful, and secure environment. Organizations have a business imperative as well as duty-of-care obligations to protect their people, along with securing facilities, valuable, and resources.

"This world of ours... must avoid becoming a community of dreadful fear and hate, and be, instead, a proud confederation of mutual trust and respect." -Dwight Eisenhower

CHAPTER 1

"Above all, I would teach him to tell the truth, Truth-telling, I have found, is the key to responsible citizenship. The thousands of criminals I have seen in 40 years of law enforcement have had one thing in common: Every single one was a liar" -J. Edgar Hoover

Criminal threats come from every direction!

EXTERNAL

Internal crimes have far greater financial impact on the organization than crimes committed by individuals outside the organization, but external crime accounts for enormous dollar losses and outsiders are more likely than insiders to perpetrate crimes of violence.

Assault (Battery)

Assault, like robbery that follows, is a crime of violence committed against the person. Assault defined: "Intentionally putting another person in reasonable apprehension of an imminent harmful or offensive contact 'With the intent to cause physical injury, actually causing such injury to another person." Protective measures, including HARDENING THE TARGET, are essentially the same as with robbery.

Bombs and Bomb Threats

Bombs and bomb threats are the preferred weapon of the terrorist. Bombs cause spectacular events resulting in the terrorist's much desired attention by the media. Bombing is relatively easy and safe for the perpetrator, who after setting a device, may simply walk away.

Due to the nature and extent of damage caused by a bomb, bombings are extremely difficult to investigate and require the services of experts, such as the Bureau of Alcohol, Tobacco, Firearms, and Explosives (BATFE), sophisticated police explosive ordinance units, and the military. Bombing is usually highly discriminate; that is, the target of a bomb is not often selected at random as in the example of a hate-based bomber selecting a house of worship as his intended target.

Bombs and bomb threats are a serious security problem. Management, especially of threatened organizations, must establish bomb threat response protocols as part of their security program at the local, regional, national, and international levels. The bomb threat policy must consider the degree of risk and danger to personnel, the consequences of damaging or destroying materials in a facility, and the total cost or loss that would result from a bombing or bomb threat. Administrators and their security providers should avail themselves of the crime prevention advisory services and resources of BATFE, FEMA, and their local police and fire departments.

Bomb Threat

The first step in responding to a bomb threat is in knowing what to do when a threat is received - the administrator and security specialist should maintain comprehensive, up-to-date reference materials, including material and information relating to bombs and bombers. BATFE; U.S. Postal Inspection Service; U.S. Customs Service, U.S. Army Ordinance Disposal, and many police departments are excellent sources of informational materials. BATFE offers a very handy pamphlet *BOMB and Physical Security Planning* that is a must-read for the security professional.

Burglary

Criminal statutes define burglary "...as the unlawful entry of, or remaining in, a structure to commit a crime therein." The degree of Burglary is categorized by a number of aggravating factors, such as armed versus unarmed, forcible entry, unlawful entry where no force is used, and attempted forcible entry. Burglary is the second most prevalent property crime in the United States.

As with most crimes, burglary is more prevalent in soft targets. Burglary is a serious felony crime that has great potential to evolve into a crime of violence against persons if unsuspecting victims are on the premises during a burglary. HARD TARGETS will reduce the burglar's opportunity and impulse to commit the crime.

The best overall strategy is to ensure that likely points of entry are safely guarded by physical and visible means of discouragement. The employment of security personnel, access and alarm systems, lights, locks, CCTV, fencing, and barriers making entry appear difficult and detection and apprehension likely is called HARDENING THE TARGET.

Security systems should make it difficult and time consuming to burglarize a building. The use of silent alarms activated by the intrusion improves the chances of apprehending the violator. Marking valuables with highly visible and unique markings makes them harder to fence, and easier to trace and identify, thus reducing its value to the intruder.

Burglars are mostly young males and can be placed into three general categories: the amateur, the semi-professional, and the professional. Amateurs comprise about 2/3rds of known burglars and are usually looking for a soft target of opportunity. Professional preventive steps will make a target too difficult for the amateur. Semi-professional burglars comprise about 1/3 of known burglars and pose the greatest immediate threat to a business. The semi-pro person will not be deterred by a weak security system of mediocre lights, locks, or alarms, and generally has ties to a fence to dispose of stolen property. Professional burglars make up less than 2% of the population of known burglars and pose the greatest long-term threat to a business. The true professional can pick locks, bypass alarms, turn off lighting systems, and open safes and is usually only interested in obtaining specific items, extremely large amounts of money, or valuable merchandise which is small in size. The professional is deterred by reducing the amount of money or merchandise available on the premises in addition to the employment of highly sophisticated security hardware. All security systems should be designed to delay the burglar, regardless of his degree of skill; the longer he is delayed, the more likely he is to go elsewhere or be discovered.

The police should be called prior to entering a building if a burglary or burglary attempt has been discovered. It may be dangerous for personnel to enter a building that could be harboring a criminal and crucial evidence needed to identify and apprehend the perpetrator may be irrevocably lost if the crime scene is compromised in any way.

Espionage and Sabotage

The loss of confidential information and valuables is a real threat to all organizations regardless of size and description. Confidential and valuable materials are defined by the organization; that is, what one large organization might deem as insignificant may very well be critically important to a smaller organization. Most organizations hold their member lists as confidential. These organizations spend time, money, and other resources developing their confidential materials and cannot afford to have them fall into the wrong hands for proprietary reasons as well as the safety and privacy of their membership. On the other end of the spectrum, confidential information such as; business plans, financial records, inventories of valuables, and the like are trade secrets and the business-backbone of the organization.

Every corporation has some trade secrets or confidential information that it must keep secure. This is much more difficult at the international level because trade secrets illegally obtained in this country may be perfectly legal and be an acceptable business practice in a foreign country that does not recognize our laws pertaining to such incidents. Espionage or sabotage maybe committed by disloyal personnel or outsiders. Multinational organizations have employees from a variety of nations, and the loyalty of such employees should be suspect when compared with loyalty for his or her native country and the culture native to the employee. Industrial espionage is easily accomplished through the use of common business equipment; computers, cameras, copiers, and electronic listening and recording devices.

Sabotage and espionage pose two major threats: (1) threats against personal safety, and (2) disruption of vital services. Sabotage may be targeted against property and may not target people. Other actions, such as arson, may directly affect human life.

Sabotage can be defined as the intentional destruction of property. The saboteur, professional or amateur, may be an internal or external threat. The saboteur may work alone or with others. Many techniques and devices may be employed to commit sabotage, including: Arson – fire and explosive devices; Mechanical Sabotage – rendering equipment and machinery inoperative by tampering or intentionally poor maintenance; Electrical & Public Utilities – interruption of electrical, water, sewage, telecommunications, and other public services; Contamination – the introduction of hazardous or toxic materials into drinking water supplies, air handling systems, fuel supplies, etc.; Psychological – disruptions based on human behaviors such as labor disputes, disorderly conduct, etc. thus creating negative situations in the workplace; Graffiti – graffiti is criminal vandalism most frequently committed by using paint, particularly spray paint, to deface property with social and political messages designed to intimidate, annoy, alarm, harass or otherwise harm or threaten the organization and its members. Sabotage and espionage are real threats and security measures must be in place to safeguard information by controlling access and preventing unauthorized duplication and dissemination.

Kidnapping and Terrorism

Terrorism and the elements of terrorism are crimes. Terrorism is the use or threatened use of force or violence used to coerce, demoralize, intimidate, or subjugate persons, organizations, businesses, or governments in order to obtain a political goal or philosophy.

Variations exist in the official definitions of terrorism between agencies. Regardless of its formal definition, terrorism, for our purpose is violence or the threat of violence against the organization or its members and assets. For many reasons, including religious, political, and financial, American organizations and businesses are prime targets of terrorist organizations in many parts of the world and more frequently here within the USA.

American organizations have been forced to establish anti-terrorist and counter-terrorist plans, which include the possibility of paying a ransom if an employee is kidnapped. Many smaller American law enforcement and security organizations are ill-equipped to adequately address Kidnap and Ransom demands or employ counter-terror tactics therefore assistance from local law enforcement agencies will be limited.

The Federal Bureau of Investigation has primary jurisdiction for kidnapping and terrorism within the United States. The U.S. State Department is the lead agency for terrorism overseas. Within the United States, the FBI has teamed with local police agencies creating anti-terrorism task forces in many cities nationwide. When pooling their resources, law enforcement agencies have been successful investigating kidnappings in the United States.

HARDEN THE TARGET - Organizations should form Safety and Security Committees with the responsibility for developing security plans and protocols and for responding to security threats against the organization.

These teams provide leadership and establish the input and direction from senior management through a liaison person to security personnel who in-turn supply expertise in resource protection and intelligence regarding security threats. The Law Department should provide legal counsel on the implications of safety and security strategies and tactics. The Finance Department should develop the financial base for the team and should record and document all expenditures. The Human Resources and Medical units provide the necessary health and biographical data on personnel and their families within the corporate framework. Senior personnel should be vested with the Media Relations responsibilities and will be called upon to provide their expertise in responding to the media and in exchanging information with the appropriate authorities.

Robbery

Criminal statutes define robbery as "... the taking or attempting to take anything of value from the care, custody, or control of a person or persons by force, threat of force or violence, or by putting the victim in fear." Please do not confuse robbery with burglary or theft – robbery is a crime of violence!

Criminologists believe that robbers plan their crimes to some extent. The robber usually wants easy money quickly and will look for a "soft target" that offers little resistance and a minimum of exposure and risk. Be reminded, it is the security function to "harden the target." Effective employment of security personnel, lighting, barriers, access systems, alarms, surveillance equipment, and other measures will result in sending a message to the would-be robber: don't do it here or you will be identified and apprehended. In other words, deny the robber the opportunity to ply his trade.

Violence is the most serious aspect of a robbery. As many as one-in-five victims of robbery suffer injury or death at the hands of robbers, most of those injured or killed offered some degree of resistance.

Organizations should provide at least a minimum of training on how to react to crime. Personnel should be instructed to do whatever it takes to stay alive. Money and merchandise has no value if you are dead. Advise the robber that you will cooperate. Remember that once a robbery is in progress, it is too late for preventive measures and the employee can't stop it. Remain as calm as possible. Concentrate on what the robber wants and what you are to do to satisfy the robber. Discreetly observe the robber and look for general characteristics of height, weight, race, sex, weapon, clothing, and mode of travel, as well as specific characteristics like tattoos, scars, missing teeth, and speech impediments. As soon as the robber has left the premises and you are safe, immediately call the police. Do not notify anyone else before calling the police.

To reduce or prevent robberies, organizations must plan and implement robbery prevention policies and procedures. Effective robbery prevention saves lives and property, and prevents serious injuries.

Theft

By their very nature many facilities are open and welcoming and thus vulnerable to the theft of small, easily concealed items thereby presenting the administrator with the balancing-act need to maintain a warm and welcoming environment while at the same time HARDENING THE TARGET.

Most thieves are amateurs who operate alone and are likely to steal as a part of a means to generate revenue while others, the more sinister thieves, may target items with a hate-based motive. Studies have shown that thieves usually operate in facilities they consider to be soft targets where personnel are not trained and are unfamiliar with security protocols.

The two most serious problems associated with theft are detecting the crime and dealing with the apprehended thief. As with all crime prevention, it is much better to have a program to reduce the opportunity for theft than to place an emphasis on the detection and apprehension of offenders. However, the detection and apprehension of violators must be a part of a comprehensive security program.

There are three times that offer opportunities for control: (1) when perpetrators enter the facility (2) when they secret the valuables, and (3) when they depart. Where appropriate, high visibility CCTV, warning signs, and electronic sensor systems should be prominent at the entrance to intimidate potential violators and reduce their capability to conceal their ill-gotten merchandise. Facilities personnel at all levels should be alert and provide discreet, courteous intervention by offering assistance to suspected persons in the vicinity of their target items. This technique puts intruders on notice that they are being observed and often causes them to leave and seek a softer target elsewhere.

When the presence of security equipment detracts from the ambiance of facilities administrators and security specialists should utilize discreet and covert security controls but in every case they must HARDEN THE TARGET.

External threats and crimes pose a greater risk of violence, injury, or death than do internal threats, and although internal threat poses a greater risk for financial harm, the safeguarding against external threats and the protection of personnel must take precedence. As organizations face increasing risk and rapidly changing technology, the preservation and protection of people, facilities, and classified information and material becomes increasingly critical.

BAD CHECKS & CREDIT CARD FRAUD

No institution is immune from these crimes

Checks

Bad checks and check fraud covers a range from accidental overdrafts against legitimate accounts to and including complex schemes to defraud, including check kiting, theft by deception, checks uttered against non-existent and fraudulent accounts, insufficient funds, forgeries, and stolen checks.

Bad-check fraud costs our nation's consumers and businesses many millions of dollars each year. The dollar amount of the fraud determines whether the offense is a misdemeanor or a felony. Prosecution of fraudulent check cases usually is based on checks uttered against non-existent and fraudulent accounts, forgeries, and stolen checks.

Institutions receiving checks on a frequent basis should implement procedures to reduce the risk of receiving bad checks. Many banks and other financial institutions provide computerized check verification machines which provide the organization with instant access to verify the transaction. The bank's phone number and the checking account number are on all checks.

Checks returned marked "no account" or "closed account" should be taken as a warning of possible fraud. Such a check is usually evidence of a fraud. If restitution is not made, prosecution would be appropriate. Forged checks are worthless, and uttering a forged check is a felony. Other alterations, illegal signatures, forgeries of the endorsement, erasures, or obliteration on genuine checks are also crimes. Dirty, damaged, and smudged checks and those with misspellings, or other irregularities should be considered suspicious.

Credit Cards

Credit card fraud perpetrated by internal and external sources is a monumental problem facing organizations today. Credit card fraud is responsible for greater losses to banks than check fraud.

Organizations that issue credit cards to their personnel should establish strict policies regarding their use and should conduct thorough credit checks on the individual before issuing a credit card. Personnel should be required to match their credit card receipts to comprehensive expense reports and to credit card company invoices and should also be required to write a brief note on the back of the credit card receipt at the time of use, to avoid a later failure to "recall" what the purchase was actually for, and to know how to post the expense: sales, entertainment, supplies, equipment, etc.

Fraudulent credit card schemes include cards illegally obtained from issuers with the intent to defraud; cards stolen from the mail, homes, offices, individuals; and using counterfeit, altered, and previously canceled cards. Credit card crimes are defined as theft and forgery and may be related to other criminal acts committed in obtaining the cards: burglary, robbery, theft, mail fraud, and others.

INTERNAL

The impact of crimes perpetrated by employees on business and other organizations has reached alarming proportions. And rest assured, when perpetrated within an organization, these losses are passed on to the members. White collar crime, including fraud and embezzlement, account for major losses in various enterprises. Without proper oversight and other safeguards, fraud frequently remains undetected until serious damage has already occurred. Far too many organizations consider internal losses as "shortages", rather than to attempt to detect and deter internal crime.

Embezzlement

Embezzlement is defined in most criminal statutes as the "fraudulent appropriation for his own use or benefit of property or money entrusted to him by another, by a clerk, agent, trustee, public officer, or other person acting in a fiduciary character." Embezzlement is a fraud perpetrated by an insider who has access to money or property and the ability to conceal the theft by "burying" it in paperwork. For example, a simple embezzlement could be the "hiding" of an unauthorized credit card purchase among many, perhaps hundreds, of legitimate receipts.

Insurance industry studies reveal that losses from embezzlement of cash reserves are seven to ten times higher than losses from property or merchandise. The administrator and security specialist must distinguish between the simple theft of property and merchandise from embezzlement. Only more-skilled thieves will be effective in large-scale embezzlement of property and only the more-skilled investigator will be qualified to investigate white collar crimes.

To reduce the risk of embezzlement, administrators and security specialists must be familiar with the human and physical elements that are generally present in perpetrating embezzlement:

Need – unusual or excessive debts may cause an employee to consider converting merchandise or money to his/her own use. Organizations should be alert to telltale signs, such as employees who live beyond their means.

Personal financial gain represents the major reason why employees steal from their employer. Because the psychological needs of individuals are difficult to discover and change over time, it is virtually impossible to identify unsatisfied needs and prevent embezzlement.

Rationalization - is the subconscious psychological state that provides explanations and excuses for one's inappropriate acts.

Rationalizations may include "I'm borrowing, not stealing", lack of moral restraint: "I can't help it", moral right: "they owe me", and reward: "I earned it."

The "borrowing, not stealing" rationalization occurs when the employee tells himself that he will return the money. Sometimes the employee may return the money in the beginning, but as the ease increases with repeated thefts, combined with growing amounts too large to repay, it becomes more unlikely that the employer can or will repay. Lack of moral restraint rationalization happens when an employee believes it is "ok" because others are doing it too. The moral right rationalization occurs when an employee believes he is only taking "what they owe me". The reward rationalization is somewhat a combination of the lack of moral restraint and the moral right rationalization; the employee sees other workers stealing and not getting caught and "believes" it is owed him anyway.

Opportunity – certain conditions must exist for the act of embezzlement to occur. Opportunity presents itself through lax or non-existent controls and procedures. Strict accountability and other controls must be in place to detect and deter embezzlement. Eliminating opportunity is the key to controlling the elements of need and rationalization. The lack of opportunity will never eliminate the need to embezzle, but it can prevent the act from happening. HARDEN THE TARGET – eliminate the opportunity!

Administrators and security personnel should be vigilant in their observation of behavioral conditions that may implicate an employee involved in embezzlement.

The most significant behavioral condition is the employee living beyond his means: making sudden changes in his/her spending habits, and making large and excessively expensive purchases (house, cars, boats, jewelry, trips, and the like). An administrator should also be aware of employees who have suffered major illness or a member of the immediate family has had such an illness and a large indebtedness incurred. All personnel who handle large amounts of money or approve purchases and vendor contracts should be observed and required to adhere to corporate policies. Personnel with fiduciary responsibilities who strongly object to procedural changes or closer supervision should be audited and observed because their resistance may be a sign of their fear of being discovered committing an illegal act.

Fraud

Fraud is defined in most criminal statutes as the "...intentional perversion of truth for the purpose of inducing another in reliance upon it to part with something of value belonging to him or to surrender a legal right."

Fraud is an essential element in various statutory offenses involving theft, misappropriation, and inventory shrinkage. "...fraud includes all acts, omissions, and concealments which involve a break of legal or equitable trust or confidence justly reposed, and are injurious to another or by which an undue or unconscionable advantage is taken of another."

Pilferage

Pilferage is the stealing of property of another in small amounts over a long period of time. Items taken are relatively inexpensive, and on a one-time basis, almost insignificant. Cumulatively, incidents of pilferage by one or more persons can amount to enormous losses to the organization.

No one actually knows how large the employee pilferage problem is or what portion of inventory shrinkage can be attributed to dishonest employees. Estimates on the number of employees who steal vary anywhere from five percent to seventy-five percent of the workforce. The opportunity to embezzle and perpetrate other frauds is restricted to a smaller number of employees therefore more employees who steal do so by committing simple acts of pilferage.

Employee pilferage schemes are likely to be simple because little planning and preparation are needed to steal company property. Studies have shown that people are more likely to steal from businesses and organizations than from other people.

Theft Control Strategies

HARDEN THE TARGET - administrators should take some action on a regular basis to detect and deter dishonest acts by employees, all personnel must be made aware that internal thefts are a serious problem and that they will not be tolerated.

To reduce losses to theft, many employers use in-house security, contract guard services, and various types of surveillance equipment. The purpose of these security measures is to eliminate the opportunity to commit theft by monitoring and restricting the movement of employees and visitors, including vendors and contractors, in and about the facility. Opportunity reduction can be accomplished through closer supervision, enforcement of procedural and access controls, increased use of security hardware devices, changes in routine, and increased emphasis on security and its importance at all levels of the work force. These protocols will HARDEN THE TARGET against internal and external attack.

The administrator should develop and implement at least the following four strategies for reducing and controlling internal theft losses: (1) screening of applicants (2) procedures or devices which make theft more difficult or apprehension easier (3) improvement in employee satisfaction and (4) the policy and process of apprehension and prosecution. Many organizations frown on strict enforcement of security programs until it's too late.

The administrator must not be swayed from recommending appropriate security measures. Remember, security is as much perception as it is a reality. Many "bosses" feel personally violated when trusted employees victimize the organization and once an organization with lax or non-existent security programs is victimized, employee morale will suffer soon thereafter.

Restoration or establishment of appropriate, not overreacting or knee-jerking, security measures must be made to return the workplace and workforce to a normal and acceptable level of comfort, productivity, and security. Once the administrator or security specialist can tactfully demonstrate to the employer what went wrong, appropriate recommendations will be more readily accepted.

Security procedures must be directed at reducing the opportunity for crime. Although some organizations question the cost involved in a solid security program they must consider that the organizational environment, regardless of its function, is not safe or secure and will not be perceived by employees to be so if it is subjected to employee-committed crime.

Security programs should be fair, equitable, and balanced to prevent negative effects on employee morale and productivity. Security programs that treat different status employees differently will soon create a negative "them-versus-us" mentality among the lower paid categories of employees and may generate the very problems they were designed to prevent.

Security programs involving apprehension and prosecution must have a solid foundation. Security personnel must be properly trained and supervised if they are to be vested with this responsibility. The rate of prosecution of employee thieves is extremely low and the decision not to prosecute is often the most appropriate but is not always up to the organization.

Prosecution by its very nature is fraught with risk. The arrest and prosecution of a high-ranking financial executive for fraud or embezzlement, for example, is a "slippery slope". Management may desire to send a message that this behavior will not be tolerated and may seek restitution. On the other hand, an arrest of this nature is likely to generate adverse press. A decision to prosecute may ultimately lead to a need to defend against libel and malicious prosecution civil suits. Additionally, other expenses related to prosecution may accrue.

CHAPTER 2

"A goal without a plan is just a wish" – Antoine de Saint-Exupery

Establishing safety and security as part of the organizational culture is crucial. The process of creating a Safety and Security Plan is accomplished in three stages: assessment, planning and implementation.

ASSESSMENT

Organizations that want to develop a Safety and Security Plan must be aware of their existing vulnerabilities so that effective safeguards can be planned. A vulnerability assessment is performed in several phases.

Police and other public safety professionals can help identify the levels and types of threat and who are most vulnerable to threats within a specific neighborhood. In addition to specific and unique threats, those targets are also susceptible to the same types of crimes that occur within the surrounding areas. Therefore working with police can help to define the nature and validity of the threats and if the threat potential is actual or perceived, and if the threat if of a physical or emotional nature. Police criminal intelligence personnel can assist in identifying potential perpetrators, times, locations, and travel routes of offenders and help identify a broad spectrum of potential threats including: natural and man-made internal and external threats.

- Coordinate with law enforcement and become aware of the crime demographics specific to the organization's neighborhood and specifically to potential threat against the organization and others at risk.

Primary concerns include vandalism, real and perceived threats, and intimidation.

- Identify and inventory target-rich assets including high-profile members, property, and valuables and develop security awareness for events and activities that may attract potential threats. Include high-profile members in your risk assessment and include private residences and other areas where high-profile members may be targeted.

- Conduct a threat assessment (risk analysis) of the primary facility and off-site locations. When conducting a threat assessment, administrators and security professionals should look beyond the obvious and be creative.

- Assess the organization's website – the organization's website is its public bulletin board and it frequently contains information equally convenient to the membership and to those who would do them harm such as: a calendar of events, photographs, scheduling, and contact information. Strategic information such as aerial photographs of the property, details of events, and the contact information of high-profile members can inadvertently render them vulnerable to abuse when such information falls into the wrong hands.

Create a Safety and Security Committee of members that includes representatives from all levels of the organization; generate buy-in of the Safety and Security Plan by your membership.

The committee should be empowered to conduct the vulnerability assessments. Such committees are the basis for establishing accountability and provide the human resources to conduct training and drills, (testing of the plan) and conducting routine inspections and maintaining the organization's safety and security mandate.

The first assessment merely identifies the types and frequencies of all natural and man-made emergencies and disasters recorded in the past in the area of the organization. If certain types of emergencies recur with regularity, predictions can be made as to the periods of the threats.

The conduct of the vulnerability assessment requires an estimation of the structural strength of the buildings of the organization to determine which of the buildings are sufficiently strong for use as shelters and which are structurally unsound and unsafe for use during natural disasters. The assessment should include an analysis of the organization's present safety and security measures.

Further risk assessment should be made to determine the extent to which the organization would be affected by a disruption in electrical, water, sewerage, and communications services, and the degree of isolation the facility would experience in event of flooded roadways, collapsed bridges or other obstructions to normal transportation. The assessment should also determine what alternate outside sources for these services would be readily available under disaster conditions, and assess those supplies available from within the organization itself.

The vulnerability assessments should result in lists of vulnerable points in the physical security of structures and surrounding areas, the maintenance of power, communications and supplies, and sustained personnel support.

The Safety and Security Committee should recommend to the facility administrator an order of priority of emergency responses to undertake under various threatening conditions. Questions such as when to order the evacuation of personnel to in-house shelters or to other safe locations should be asked.

There must be a pre-established set of conditions and instructions prepared to cover any emergency. There should be limited personal discretion allowed for personnel involved in emergency operations.

PLANNING

Once you have identified the types, levels, and locations of the threats it is time to begin developing the Safety and Security Plan. Your plan should include the following:

• Define counter-measures to potential threats within practical and financial limits. Developing the plan is a balancing act that calls for tailoring the individual plan to address defined risk areas and known and perceived threats while recognizing the unique culture of the organization - this balance will provide the greatest results.

• The plan should provide recommendations to HARDEN THE TARGET.

• The budget must be realistic - remember somebody has to pay for this. The plan should include creative alternatives to provide for safety and security as well as finding creative ways to pay for it.

The only thing certain about planning to protect lives or property from natural or man-made emergencies or disasters is that there is no location, anywhere in the world, that is absolutely free from danger in one form or another. The varieties of potential dangers can be identified and measures can be taken to reduce the risk of exposure to those dangers by people or property.

The planning to cope with emergencies or disasters should begin with a mandate by high-ranking representatives of the organization and expanded to include the Safety and Security Committee. The planning committee should not be too large or agreements will be difficult to reach, but it should be large enough to ensure representation from all segments of the organization. Someone with knowledge of the security field, whether a staff member who has the responsibility for security or an outside security consultant, should be on the committee. However, the security manager should not be appointed as the committee head or sole investigator, unless he holds high position of authority within the organization. The following factors should be included in the planning process for an emergency and disaster control plan.

Authority

The owner, manager, or governing body of an organization should prepare a simple, written order to authorize the committee to develop the emergency control plan. The order should provide the committee with the necessary authority to develop a written plan, and then organize, train, and assign responsibilities to an emergency force within the organization. This statement should be brief and flexible so that the committee can adjust its deliberations as necessary. Existing organizational rules and regulations will have to be researched to ensure that there is not already an emergency plan that has been overlooked or forgotten.

Written authority should exist to organize certain personnel into a special force during declared emergencies. There may be personnel occupying certain responsible positions who would object to such an extra assignment, or who might be physically or emotionally unsuited for assignment to an emergency force. For this reason an effort should be made to attract volunteers from the organization for the emergency force. Consideration for assignment to the force should be given to persons with unusual abilities and special interests that would be of benefit.

Personnel selected for the emergency force should undergo training in primary and alternate emergency duties. Cross-training the emergency force allows for a greater range of assignments and for the assumption of responsibilities in the event that another member is absent or becomes incapacitated.

The order of authority should also provide a chain of command that specifies the individuals who have the authority to order certain activities or changes, or assume leadership roles in the event that higher ranking personnel are unavailable during an emergency.

Appointment of the Safety and Security Coordinator

Large organizations may have the resources to appoint a full-time coordinator to manage the development or implementation of the plan. In smaller organizations someone may have to assume this role part time. The coordinator should be of sufficient authority within the organization so he will be able to deal effectively with others at all levels in the organization. The coordinator understand the value of preparedness and he must generate support for the program during periods when there appears that there is little or no threat.

The appointment of the coordinator signals that top management fully supports the project.

Use of In-House Personnel

Regardless of the size of the organization, presently employed and volunteer personnel should perform the majority, if not all, of the necessary emergency duties.

The nucleus of the emergency organization can be those personnel already trained and utilized to perform routine and emergency services, such as the foremen, supervisors, and other key administrative personnel, as well as the existing medical, fire, safety and security staff. Other emergency response personnel can be selected from the regular employees and members who have demonstrated special talents or interests.

As the Safety and Security Plan develops, other persons may be found to have special skills or an interest in training to acquire additional skills that would contribute to the emergency response effort.

Sources of Assistance

Planning must also incorporate as much self-help as possible during such emergencies to minimize the cost to the organization.

Self-help

An important aspect of the vulnerability assessment is to identify the activities and material that are presently located within the surveyed facility.

Not only must the regular employees be selected and trained for their responsive roles but any material or supplies such as: food, water, tools, portable equipment, lumber, or other property that could be used to protect or repair the facility or to recover from interrupted services must be inventoried and kept in serviceable condition. The vulnerability assessment should also estimate the amount of emergency supplies (sandbags, plywood, nails, etc.) that would be necessary in the event that a certain building or facility had to be protected or occupied throughout an emergency. Many organizations will have within their facilities supplies that could be utilized as makeshift material to block doors and windows, provide a limited water supply, or serve as emergency rations.

Government and public services

It may be surprising but even organizations that prepare emergency plans often do not take advantage of available government information on the subject. The Safety and Security Planning Committee should contact the various government agencies that can provide this assistance, among them are:

- The Federal Emergency Management Agency (2400 M Street NW, Washington, DC 20472) provides published information and recommendations on how to counteract and minimize losses caused by enemy action, natural or man-made disasters. That office should be contacted for an up-to-date bibliography of related U.S. Government Printing Office publications.

- Regional emergency and disaster agencies can provide additional information that may have a more local orientation concerning emergencies that are most likely to occur.

As the local coordinating agency for emergency and disaster situations, they can also provide recommendations for local responses to ensure the fullest cooperation and protective measures appropriate to the area.

- State and local governments provide police, fire, and other services, including environmental protection, health and welfare and many more services during normal periods as well as during emergency conditions.

- Public utility and public service agencies may provide water, electricity, telephone communications, sanitation and other services. These agencies should be contacted to learn how they plan to continue their services during an emergency.

Not every police, fire department or other agency will be able to provide all the services requested. For that reason, it is the planning committee's responsibility to establish exactly what services would be available during various emergency situations, and acquire information on how alternative services can be obtained and to develop strong relationships with their police and fire departments.

One problem frequently overlooked in emergency planning is the identification of employees with unusual health or disability impairments. There are many people in the general population who require constant medical attention, medication and clinical services. Those persons handicapped by severe color or night blindness, diabetes or epilepsy, for instance, may not only be unable to contribute to emergency functions, but may require special help and attention themselves during the emergency.

Therefore, such people should provide instructions as to how they might be helped (name and phone number of physician, medication source, etc.) in the event their malady is aggravated during an emergency.

The vulnerability surveys should have determined the areas with a need for additional personnel support during emergencies. There are several ways to increase personnel strengths from within the organization. One way is to eliminate or decrease non-critical activities and reassign those personnel temporarily. Another way would be to reduce administrative staffs by deferring or postponing non-essential duties until after the emergency subsides. A third way would be to solicit spouses and relatives of present employees to either contribute their services or to accept temporary employment. The employment of additional personnel, from among people with a vested interest in the organization, may be more productive and involve less risk than hiring outsiders who would have no loyalty for the organization.

Developing the Plan

The existing organizational structure should be utilized as much as practicable for the emergency plan.

The regular supervisory authority, the technical skills, the equipment and material at hand and familiar to the employees should form the foundation for emergency actions. In this respect, the disaster organization will not be seen as a separate entity and possibly as a threat by the remainder of the organization. The following factors should be considered in the development of the disaster plan.

- The conditions requiring the activation of the emergency or disaster control program should be listed.

- The person or persons with the authority to declare an emergency should be identified.
- Maps and blueprints of the facility to be protected should be provided.
- An emergency control center and an alternate site should be designated.
- Communications facilities between the control center, the major sections of the facility, and the community should be established. Alternate means of communication (radios, sound-powered phones, etc.) should be provided.
- An emergency organization hierarchy should be developed and a list of employees and their emergency duties should be available.
- Emergency shut-down procedures should be developed, and lists made of critical property and records to be secured.
- Emergency evacuations should be planned.
- Shelters should be identified and supplied with food, medical supplies, water, and disaster equipment.
- An augmented security force should be planned.
- Damage assessment and repair teams should be designated.
- Emergency power, fuel and utilities should be ready to be activated as needed.
- Plans for cooperation with federal, state and local police, fire and emergency preparedness officials should be developed. Mutual aid pacts should be set up.
- Records should be kept of all activities that take place during the emergency for satisfaction of legal liabilities and possible later revision of the disaster plan.

A sound Safety and Security Plan is the result of thorough advance planning, testing, revision, and updating. An adequate emergency plan must contain detailed and timely information about the resources that can be utilized in the most efficient and expeditious manner. The plan for emergency control must consider the goals and personnel that comprise the organization. Emergency planning must be a continuing process if the best safeguards possible are expected and all planned emergency control measures must be arranged so that they complement and supplement each other. Poorly integrated emergency control measures result in the waste of manpower, funds, and equipment and the lack of integration in the plans may jeopardize the safety and security of the facility.

The Role of Security

The establishment or engagement of security forces should be considered by management and the planning committee. Emergency planning for any type of organization entails the orderly and efficient transition from normal to emergency operations by the regular work force. The energy and power of the regular work force is many times greater than the security personnel could provide. Still, the role of security is crucial in that a greater degree of protection must be provided in a period of crisis.

IMPLEMENTATION

When Implementing your Safety and Security Plan ensure that everyone in the organization is included and then communicate, coordinate, and cooperate! Establish an open and an ongoing dialogue within the organization and solicit feedback and remember that security is as much a perception as it is a reality.

The membership needs to be involved in implementation just as they are in the planning stage. Assigning members the responsibility of implementation reinforces the feeling of partnership in the process thereby generating more good will and buy-in with the plan. Assigned responsibilities frequently include: training the volunteer staff to recognize and report suspicious activities and persons; patrolling the facilities regularly; maintaining emergency contact information; scheduling safety and security workshops; and conducting efficiency drills.

All plans will become stale overtime unless they are maintained and updated – safety and security is no exception. Create a schedule to regularly conduct drills, validate procedures, improve training and examine facilities and in so doing you will ensure that your safety and security plan remains effective.

Testing the Plan

When the plan has been completed, provisions for its implementation and testing must be made. This is the time when deficiencies and unrealistic features of the plan are discovered and corrected.

CHAPTER 3

"Precaution is better than cure" – Edward Coke

The tragedy of 9/11 changed America and security in America forever. Crime statistics indicate that Americans are confronted by social and cultural problems including Hate-Based crimes against individuals and organizations based on bias, ignorance and intolerance. The evils of Hate-Crime threaten the safety and security of all people, homes, and places of worship and business in the United States and Americans traveling abroad.

We are all responsible for preventing and deterring crime and criminality and to appreciate the role of security in America one must understand the tasks it faces. All threats to security can be classified into one of two broad categories: Manmade and Natural.

MANMADE HAZARDS

Manmade hazards come in two forms: intentional and accidental actions and it is often difficult to ascertain if an occurrence was intentional, accidental, or the result of a natural phenomenon.

The most common and devastating types of hazards are fire and crime. Fire can be the byproduct of intentional, accidental, and natural occurrences. Crime, as we know, is manmade. Criminal culpability in a particular situation will be determined through investigation and the judicial process.

Crime

Crime is a principal threat facing all Americans. In order to detect and deter crime and criminality, we must understand its intensity and know the threat environment, the criminal, and the roles society plays in its occurrence and prevention.

Crimes are divided into two basic types: crimes against persons or crimes of violence and crimes against property.

Crimes against persons include the violence of murder, kidnapping, rape, assault, and robbery. Crimes against property include burglary, arson, vandalism, sabotage, shoplifting, and theft. In considering crimes such as arson we clearly see that property crimes can, and often do, take a turn to violence. Crimes are classified by their severity as misdemeanors or felonies. A misdemeanor is usually defined as a crime with a penalty of a fine, a jail sentence of up to a year, or both. The penalties for a felony range from fines, one or more years or in prison, or the death penalty.

GENERAL DESCRIPTIONS – CRIMES

Crimes are defined as felonies and misdemeanors; although often found within criminal statutes, such lesser infractions as violations and offenses are not crimes.

In protecting the facility and thus their people, administrators and security personnel must first understand that the means by which crimes are perpetrated are varied and complex and they must also understand that it is their responsibility to reduce the risks of victimization by being aware of the myriad factors involved.

They should be aware of their surroundings including the people, places, and things that constitute their local and extended neighborhoods. They must become familiar with the nearness and responsiveness of police and fire protection and the types of protective hardware and procedures available to them and they must be fully engaged in deterring criminal attacks.

There will always be some deviant behavior in every society. However, crime can be reduced if effective and efficient measures are taken to deter and detect crime or deny access to those activities that are detrimental, in other words, HARDEN THE TARGET.

The Criminal

Criminals are not readily identifiable by their ethnicity, race, religion, appearance, speech, manner, background, attitude, behavior, skills, or method of criminal operation. There are however some factors that can be utilized to identify the criminal and detect or deter his attempts to commit a crime. Administrators and their security professionals must develop good working relationships with area law enforcement agencies and they must follow the adage "if you see something report it." Criminal intelligence agencies monitor the activities of known and suspected felons, terrorists, and those who plot hate-crimes. Often the first line of defense against the criminal is a combination of Target Hardening and effective Criminal Intelligence.

There is no such thing as a "typical criminal" each person acts and reacts according to his or her own inherent and acquired characteristics and capabilities. The security professional must be aware of his or her surroundings, have a thorough knowledge of the elements of crime, and understand the various Modus Operandi (MO) employed by criminals.

The primary objective of most criminals is personal or financial gain, not necessarily so with haters and terrorists who are motivated by, well, hate, yet still they commit financial and other crimes. Accordingly, theft related crimes are the most frequent and account for a good deal of the prevention and detection responsibilities of the security professional. Less common criminal activities, but of equal or greater concern, include the destruction of property and crimes against persons – the violent crimes.

MOST CRIMINALS AVOID HARD TARGETS because they do not want to get caught. Soft targets, targets of opportunity, for robbery, burglary and other crimes exist where it is readily apparent to the criminal that his goals are easily attainable, victims are relatively unprotected, and that there is little danger of being detected or apprehended.

Although some professional or career criminals earn a living from criminal activity, most crimes are committed by amateur criminals on the spur of the moment as the opportunity presents itself. Criminologists estimate that professional criminals account for only a small percentage of the total criminal population. Amateurs commit most crimes and most crimes are crimes of opportunity. Crime statistics show that more than fifty percent of those arrested for criminal acts are juveniles.

The professional criminal makes a living through crime, usually one specific crime or specialty. He likely began his career as an amateur, but was able, through luck or ability, to develop his skills to the point of being a successful criminal. He usually develops a "refined" MO.

Given the time and proper conditions, a highly skilled and determined professional criminal can successfully penetrate nearly any protective system. In addition to deterring the criminal, it is of great importance to inconvenience and interfere with his progress. The longer it takes a criminal to perpetrate his crime the more likely he is to be discovered, when threat of discovery becomes too severe the criminal will see the target as being too "hard." Once deterred he will likely seek "softer targets." Facilities well secured by strong locks and other perimeter barriers, effective lighting, and protected by alarm systems and CCTV will deter most criminals, amateur or professional.

To effectively protect their areas of responsibility, the administrator and security specialist must view the belongings as though he himself were a criminal looking for a target and as if they were the detectives investigating the ensuing crime. The combined views from the perspectives of both the criminal and the investigator should reveal the weaknesses and the strengths of existing security measures. The security professional should have knowledge of the methods and techniques utilized by criminals to commit crimes if effective countermeasures are to be taken.

Sadly, many criminal activities are perpetrated from within the environment to be protected - this is known as the "internal threat." Administrators and security specialists must evaluate their protection needs from both perspectives; internal and external.

It is your job to HARDEN THE TARGET!

To be complete, security must be approached systematically. Analyzing the threats; whether internal or external, manmade, or natural, is your first step in providing effective preventive or deterrent action. Recent developments and technological advances have greatly enhanced advance warnings of adverse conditions. With in-depth planning and adequate preparation, property losses and life-threatening events can be reduced. The professional security manager must be proficient in the application of the National Incident Management System and the Incident Command System both managed by the Federal Emergency Management Agency.

Fire and Life Safety

Each year fires in the United States claim thousands of victims, injure thousands more, and cause billions of dollars in property loss and damage and are responsible for severe losses of jobs, customers, employees and businesses. The National Fire Protection Association provides: "fire is more related to human acts of omission and commission than to science and there is no denying that people cause most fires and that most 'people-caused' fires are due to thoughtless acts of carelessness than from any uncontrolled interactions of reactive materials." Fire is most frequently the result of human acts or neglect, such as poor housekeeping, careless use of smoking materials, inadequate or improper construction, improper utilization and maintenance of equipment, and intentional acts of arson and sabotage. The human element in fire is far more prevalent than natural environmental influences.

As an integral part of the security service, fire prevention programs must include a comprehensive analysis of the hazardous materials and operations that are common to the environment within your areas or responsibility. Disaster analysis must be used in developing effective fire safety rules and regulations.

Most fires are the result of human error and therefore are frequently preventable. Discipline, training, and education are the keys to fire prevention. Fire safety and prevention programs beginning in pre-school, elementary and secondary schools, and continuing to the workplace are essential. Safety programs, including drills and training, should be mandatory for all employees of an organization – no one, regardless of position within the organization, should be exempt from being fully informed of the importance and techniques of fire safety. Rules and regulations regarding fire safety should be common knowledge to every employee. These standards should be strictly enforced.

The threat of fire cannot be totally eliminated and must not be underestimated. Therefore, a realistic goal of fire prevention should be set while establishing comprehensive emergency response plans. Security plays a vital role in life-safety services, including fire prevention and control.

NATURAL HAZARDS

Natural hazards present unique and challenging situations to manage. When a natural disaster strikes, it also strikes public safety, security, emergency medical, and other professionals, their homes and families, as well. Some natural occurrences are more common to some areas of the United States than others. The following list represents some of the more common natural hazards and where they are most likely to occur:

- Earthquakes - Most common to the Pacific coast
- Tidal Waves or Tsunami - Coastal areas
- Floods – Coastal, low-lying, and waterway areas
- Fire, Lightning - Anywhere in U.S.

- Storm - Hurricane (coastal areas), Tornado (anywhere in U.S.), Snow and ice (anywhere in U.S. except extreme southern areas), High winds (anywhere in U.S.), and temperature extremes (anywhere in U.S.)

Modern climatology and meteorology have made many natural hazards more predictable. It is often possible to receive advance warning and some indication of the probable magnitude of a pending hazard. Unfortunately, many natural hazards still strike without warning; it is then that pre-planning and immediate and adequate reaction capabilities are of the utmost importance. Contingency and protection plans for emergency personnel, facilities, and equipment must also be made. You can't respond if you lose your people and material in the disaster.

Although it is impossible to prevent such natural disasters, there are steps that can be taken to minimize loss of life and property. First, choose a site for the facility where such disasters are rare. Second, construct a facility that will withstand anticipated natural hazards. Third, develop emergency plans to reduce the damage that such disasters can cause. And finally, create mutual assistance programs so that others may be capable of responding to your problems and you to theirs. This will require cross-training and the establishment of effective communications as well as other planning measures which will be included in your overall security protocol.

"The safety of the people must be the supreme law" – Roman Proverb

CHAPTER 4

"Terrorism is a psychological warfare. Terrorists try to manipulate us and change our behaviour by creating fear, uncertainty, and division in society." - Patrick J. Kennedy

Hate-crime, the violence of extremism, is born of intolerance and fueled by bigotry. The disparity between terrorism and hate-crime is a difference without a distinction. Like its cousin terrorism, hate-crimes are intended to intimidate. The purveyors of hate use violence and the threat of violence to achieve their objectives and they employ a full-range of criminal activity and weaponry in their fetid quest including; arson, explosives, weapons, vandalism, and physical violence, and verbal threats of violence to instill fear in their victims and to make them vulnerable to future attacks. The security measures found within this chapter have application to detecting and deterring such crimes.

To provide effective countermeasures against terrorist attacks, we must first understand precisely what we are talking about. Unfortunately, as is often the case within the federal bureaucracy, there are as many definitions of terrorism as there are agencies charged with combating it. Research reveals more than 100 definitions of terrorism - the following definitions are provided by the United States Department of State (DOS) and the Federal Bureau of Investigation (FBI) to illustrate my point:

DOS

"No one definition of terrorism has gained universal acceptance.

'For the purposes of this report, however, we have chosen the definition of terrorism contained in Title 22 of the United States Code, Section 2656f(d).' That statute contains the following definitions:"

- The term "terrorism" means premeditated, politically motivated violence perpetrated against noncombatant targets by subnational groups or clandestine agents, usually intended to influence an audience.

- The term "international terrorism" means terrorism involving citizens or the territory of more than one country.

- The term "terrorist group" means any group practicing, or that has significant subgroups that practice, international terrorism."

FBI

"The unlawful use of force or violence against persons or property to intimidate or coerce a Government, the civilian population, or any segment thereof, in furtherance of political or social objectives"

The word "terrorism" is emotionally charged and politically controversial. In considering hate-crimes and the tragedy of September 11, 2001, it is safe to assume we all hold our own definitions of terrorism and our own strong beliefs on what ought to be done about it.

Terrorists – who are they? Loosely defined, terrorists are crazies, criminals, or crusaders. Criminals: certainly the conduct of any terrorist act is criminal in nature. Crusaders: no one is more dedicated than the religious zealot or the bias-based hater.

A common definition: "Terrorism is the systematic use of terror, especially as a means of coercion. At present, the international community has been unable to formulate a universally-agreed, legally binding criminal-law definition of terrorism. Common definitions of terrorism refer only to those violent acts which are intended to create fear, are perpetrated for an ideological goal, and deliberately target or disregard the safety of civilians."

OK where do we go from here? Of course the simple answer is to counter terrorism; however, this is an extremely complex problem requiring a complex, sophisticated, comprehensive, and coordinated response. As we've seen above, we can't get agencies to use the same language, let alone fully and openly Communicate, Coordinate, and Cooperate.

COUNTER-TERRORISM

Counterterrorism plans, programs, and protocols include the deterrence and detection of terrorist acts and the response to related events. It is the proactive strategies, tactics, practices, tools, and techniques that governments, militaries, police departments, security agencies, and corporations employ to prevent or respond to terrorist threats or actions actual, planned, or perceived.

ANTI-TERRORISM

The Department of Defense (DOD) defines antiterrorism as "defensive measures used to reduce the vulnerability of individuals and property to terrorist acts." DOD makes a distinction between counterterrorism, which are offensive measures taken to prevent, deter, and respond to terrorism and the defensive measures of antiterrorism. Both are part of the DOD force-protection protocol that assembles all protective measures in a broader program of DOD personnel and assets, in any event, both call for the "hardening" of security.

An abstract from the American Society of Criminology notes that "...prior to September 11, 2001, private security was, at best, a deterrent to crime, often used as a form of crime prevention. Many of the individuals who work within this industry were not required, nor had any desire, to perform functions in-line with law enforcement officers. However, after 9/11 they were thrust into America's war on terrorism, as a number of private security firms have become active agents in the domestic war on terror. When properly trained, private security officers can be a useful force against threats of terror..."

The following is adapted from a speech given Charles P. Connolly at the National Executive Institute Associates, Major Cities Chiefs Association, and Major County Sheriff's Association Annual Conference at Sun Valley, Idaho. Mr. Connolly was Assistant Commissioner of the New York City Police Department, Chief of the Yonkers, NY, Police Department, and vice president in charge of security for Merrill Lynch Corporation.

"All disasters are essentially local. There is no such thing as a Homeland Security Department disaster or an FBI disaster, there are only; New York City, Los Angeles, Chicago, or even Des Moines disasters. Yes, their impact matters and relates to the larger community. If we are to be successful in developing a more productive antiterrorist environment, both the public police sector and the private security sector need to change their client culture from one of mere security awareness or knowledge to that of security ownership and responsibility."

"Darkness cannot drive out darkness; only light can do that. Hate cannot drive out hate; only love can do that" - Martin Luther King, Jr.

CHAPTER 5

"Rather fail with honor than succeed by fraud" - Sophocles

The basis of an effective fraud-prevention program is the pro-active development, implementation, and enforcement of internal controls.

Proactive fraud-prevention programs and reactive-detection methodologies are the vanguards of healthy fiscal management. The risks of failing to establish controls, policies, and procedures are numerous and dangerous. First, consider the impact on the bottom line, and remember when we are talking about fiduciary responsibility, it's always about the bottom line. Second, the impact of negative publicity on organizations can be very damaging and embarrassing. Executives don't want people reading about fraud in the organization on the front page of the *Wall Street Journal*. Finally, organizations may incur vicarious or imputed liability and be held responsible for acts of their employees.

All organizations should implement-fraud prevention and detection programs, the sooner the better!

Finance Officers, internal and external auditors, account managers, legal counsel, human resources personnel, corporate security, and investigators alike should receive training in fraud prevention and reaction.

Fraud Control

No security plan is complete without addressing the problematic areas of fraud, waste and abuse. The fraud prevention survey is complete when the security specialist or auditor can answer the following questions affirmatively or assist the organization in initiating solutions to negative responses.

NOTE: The items audited are rated in one of the following three categories:
1. Unacceptable
2. Acceptable (meets standards)
3. Exceeds Standards

The first step in reducing internal fraud is to establish a pre-employment screening program whereby background investigations are conducted on applicants:

- Does organization have a pre-employment screening program in place?
- Is a signed and completed application received from each applicant for employment containing an Authorization for Release of Information and Records?
- Are applications for employment reviewed for completeness?
- Do applications contain verbiage to the effect that falsification of the application may result in automatic disqualification?
- Are in-depth one on one interviews conducted with all applicants?
- Are criminal records checks conducted on all final applicants?
- Are credit checks conducted on all final applicants?
- Are previous employers contacted prior to making an offer of employment?

- Are applicants questioned about all periods of self-employment and unexplained periods of time between jobs?
- Are periods of self-employment verified through tax records?
- Are education and military service verified?
- Are applicant drivers licenses verified against the information listed on the employment application?
- Is drug testing conducted on all final applicants?
- Does the organization have guidelines of areas of automatic disqualification?
- Are personnel files audited periodically for compliance?
- Are discrepancies reported and corrected per company policy?
- Does the organization maintain a database on former employees ineligible for rehire?

Establish internal controls to reduce the likelihood of fraud within an organization:

- Is there a formal hierarchy structure within the organization?
- Is someone designated the responsibility of loss prevention matters?
- Does the individual report to somebody outside of operations?
- Is there at least one individual responsible for audit duties?
- Does the individual(s) responsible for conducting audits report to somebody outside of operations, where a possible conflict could present?
- Are there adequate proactive internal controls in place to combat fraud?
- Who is tasked with ensuring compliance with the various controls?
- Are disbursement procedures in place, updated, and followed?

- Are controls in place to ensure that adequate documentation accompanies paperwork relating to disbursements?
- Are physical security controls in place to protect assets?
- Is there a secure access system, are limits set to block access to restricted areas?
- Has the organization taken a proactive role in reducing fraud?
- Are employees who are not working restricted from the office or other areas where business is being conducted?
- Are relatives prohibited from working together within the same department?
- Are spot checks and random audits conducted?
- Is there an employee fraud-prevention training program?
- Is there an anonymous fraud, waste and abuse hotline or other mechanism whereby employees can report violations?
- Is there a reward program to encourage employees to report fraud?
- Are audits conducted periodically in various departments to ensure compliance with policy and to evaluate operational efficiency?
- Are random audits performed as a deterrent to fraudulent practices?
- Are employees required to take vacation leave?
- Is there a random drug testing policy?
- Is there an open door policy to report fraud or suspected fraud?
- Is suspicious customer behavior brought to the attention of a supervisor?
- Is CCTV or other electronic security capability employed?
- Is access limited within the company? How?
- Is failure to report a dishonest act a violation of company policy in and of itself?

Controls should be established that will reduce the probability of fraud perpetrated by vendors with and without collusion from an internal source such as:

- Is there an approved vendor list?
- Is the vendor list updated annually by senior management?
- Is vendor selection reviewed and approved by the respective department heads?
- Is a due diligence investigation conducted on prospective vendors?
- Is there a computerized purchase order systems?
- Are there controls in place over vendor lists?
- Are department heads required to approve purchases over a set limit?
- Are receiving reports matched to purchase orders, vendor invoices, and inventory prior to entry in the payables system?
- Is supporting documentation attached to the vendor checks for review by the controller?
- Are checks and supporting documentation forwarded to the general manager for signature after review by controller?
- Are two signatures required on company checks over a set amount?
- Is there an established check cashing policy within the organization?
- Are there adequate controls of keys and safes to guard against unauthorized access?

Handling bank deposits and settlements:

- Are only essential personnel present?
- Are settlements and counting of bank deposits kept secret?
- Are distractions kept at a minimum?
- Is cash safeguarded from exposure to view?

- Does a manager maintain control of the environment?
- Is the office properly secured during settlements?
- Are bills of $10 or higher checked with counterfeit pens?
- Are counterfeit bills reported to a supervisor and police?
- Are deposits verified by a second employee?
- Are settlements recorded and reviewed when there are unresolved discrepancies?
- Is management notified of all account deposit discrepancies?
- Is a safe-deposit log maintained and reviewed by accounting?
- Is the deposit summary forwarded to audit or accounting daily?
- Are the summaries reviewed by audit or accounting on a daily basis?
- Is cash prevented from accumulating in the safe?
- Are deposits made daily?
- Are times, routes, and routines of deposits varied?
- Are deposits made by two or more employees?
- Are bank deposit bags concealed when being transported to the bank?

Wire Transfers:

- Is there an established a policy regarding wire transfers?
- Is there a dedicated person within the organization to handle such transfers?
- Are all transfers approved by the department head?
- Do all wire transfers require two signatures?
- Are such transfers reviewed weekly by audit to ensure compliance with policy?

- Are irregularities reported to the controller or designated individual?

Factors to help detect and deter Check and Credit Card Fraud:

- Are internal controls in-place to detect and prevent fraud?
- Are proper forms of ID required and expiration date checked?
- Are IDs examined for suspicious or unusual markings?
- Are credit cards and checks examined for alterations?
- Is unusual or suspicious behavior noted regarding the presenter of the checks and credit cards?
- Is the acceptance of third party checks prohibited?
- Are pre-printed names and addresses required on checks received?
- Are personal and pre- or post-dated checks declined?
- Are checks made payable to "cash" or "bearer" declined?
- Are personal checks of employees declined?
- Do signatures on credit cards match those on the sales slips? (probably the single most important action in deterring credit card fraud)
- When credit cards are not signed, is a driver's license or state-issued ID required and checked to verify identification?
- Are expiration dates checked on credit cards?
- Are holograms checked to ensure they are clear, distinct, and undamaged?
- Are credit cards checked to ensure the magnetic strips are intact?
- Are account numbers matched to those of the point-of-sales printouts?

- Are card issuers notified of suspicious actions by card presenters?
- When notified of a stolen credit card by the issuer, does the employee contact a supervisor to deal with seizure of the card?
- Are police contacted whenever a stolen credit card is presented?

Investigating Check and Credit Card Fraud:

- Are there known or suspected incidents of preventable check and/or credit card fraud?
- Are supervisors made aware of suspected fraud?
- Is there is a reporting protocol to account for and report fraud?
- Are cases of check and credit card fraud reported to police?
- Are police case numbers are always obtained?
- Are such cases are reported to the card issuer?
- Is prosecution routinely sought?

Computer Security:

- Are unique passwords required to access all computer applications?
- Are passwords required to be alpha-numeric characters?
- Are passwords changed frequently?
- Is virus protection installed on the network file server?
- Are individual company computers protected with anti-virus protection?
- Are computer data files backup procedures in-place?
- Is a complete system backup performed with adequate frequency?
- Are backup files stored in a fireproof lockbox?
- Are backup files maintained offsite?

- Is the sharing of passwords prohibited?
- Is there a comprehensive 'company' computer use policy?
- Is the computer use policy consistent with the security plan?
- Who handles the IT responsibilities?
- If IT matters are contracted, has the vendor been properly vetted?
- Is the IT firm licensed and bonded?

Resignations and terminations:

- Are IDs, keys and pass cards retrieved from those leaving the 'company?'
- Are sincere exit interviews conducted with all departing employees?
- Is information related to possible fraud obtained during exit interviews and conveyed to the person responsible for security and loss-prevention?
- Do termination procedures include prosecution for fraud when applicable? (employees must have some fear of the consequences of their actions otherwise there is little to no deterrent to fraud)
- Are locks and safe combinations changed?
- Is the alarm company notified to remove former associates from the emergency call list, invalidate employee's access code(s), and remove the card from the card access system?
- Are the banks and other financial institutions notified?

CHAPTER 6
Protecting the Perimeter

"Against danger it pays to be prepared" - Aesop

The ability to protect and secure any facility or building largely depends upon the environment or general location of the structure, the area immediately surrounding the facility must be secure if the facility itself is to remain secure.

The first line of physical defense is the perimeter. It is here that we most desire to deter the criminal, prevent intrusion, and record his activities. Perimeter security is accomplished by the effective employment of alarms, access systems, CCTV, barriers, and lighting, the security design of the structure itself, and the posting of guards.

The facilities of the targets of hate, including houses of worship, are for the most part warm, welcoming, and open and therefore more difficult to secure. The more accessible a facility, the more vulnerable it becomes. As security measures are increased, vulnerability decreases with resultant increases in cost to management, increases and inconvenience to congregants, employees, and management. Efforts to secure a facility perimeter largely depend upon why it is being secured and frequently creates a "balancing act" requiring tradeoffs in terms of the quality and quantity of security with regard to costs, inconvenience, and aesthetic qualities. The selection and deployment of security services and personnel are therefore, usually dependent upon the perception of costs, needs and utility of action.

Site Layout

Retrofitting older existing facilities with state-of-the-art security is challenging, however new, often wireless, and ever evolving technology is proving to be advantageous in such applications. The employment of a combination of overt, discreet, and covert equipment will provide a multi-layered security shield – for a visual, think about the greatest museums with the most incredible collections and exhibits you've ever visited, they utilize such layered security.

Securing new facilities is much easier and far more cost-effective when security is part of the initial building plan.

Frequently, security is the last concern or totally disregarded during the planning and construction of a facility. Management and real estate divisions are often more interested in other requirements such as location as it pertains to easy access, economy of construction and operation, convenience, and other issues. Sometimes, it is only after construction has begun or the facility put into operation that management considers security – in some instances, security technology isn't even included in the building's blueprints or other specifications. By this time, the security problems are much harder to address – it is not uncommon to see perfectly good, brand new construction demolished or modified to facilitate the installation of security systems because security was an afterthought. To properly, effectively, and efficiently provide security; security specialists should have input from the initial architectural planning stages through building completion. This will facilitate appropriate compromise between cost, convenience and security issues. If adequate attention is not given to security during the planning stages, then security costs or loss and shrinkage will probably increase and are likely to out-weigh any earlier perceived savings.

Security planning begins with regard to site layout and the positioning of the facility on the building lot. Care should be exercised to ensure that the building/s receives maximum exposure from adjacent thoroughfares. The more isolated a building, the more vulnerable it will be to unauthorized access and egress. A Law Enforcement Assistance Administration study showed that over 2/3rds of the burglaries reported in selected areas of California, the points of entry were not visible. Likewise, robberies increase in locales with limited visibility and poor lighting. Would-be robbers tend to select targets in areas where they are likely to avoid detection.

When feasible, it is generally best to situate a building in the middle of the lot to facilitate movement around the facility and aid in observation. When this is not possible and a structure is located adjacent to another structure, additional security measures must be taken to protect against unauthorized access and egress.

With proper planning, installation, and maintenance, landscaping should also play an important role in crime prevention. Desires to make the facility as attractive as possible can be balanced with security needs. The introduction of shrubbery, trees and other vegetation or ornamentation must be carefully planned. Without the proper consideration, landscaping can compromise security. If possible, the size and placement of vegetation should be located 50 or more feet from the structure. This will increase visibility and help deter illegal activities by eliminating or limiting the concealment of would-be perpetrators.

Planning and care should also be taken with regard to where and how equipment, products, supplies and materials enter and leave the facility. These areas should remain free from obstruction to decrease the possibility of employees or carriers secreting goods and merchandise and later retrieving them. This is especially important around loading docks, mail rooms, and rail entrances.

"Hardscaping" including ornamental fencing, lighting, fountains, etc. are an integral part of landscaping that is used to beautify and when properly planned, can be of benefit to the security program. Frequently the benefits of lighting are lost when used for advertisement or other purposes without regard to security – lighting can and should include security.

To be efficient and cost effective, security planning should be early and continuous throughout the construction or remodeling process. Structures and perimeter areas should not only be pleasing to the eye, but also designed and constructed to reduce their vulnerability to illegal activity.

Physical Barriers

There are two basic types of barriers, natural and manmade. Natural barriers include geographical obstacles such as rivers, lakes, mountains, cliffs, deserts, canyons, swamps, or other types of terrain. Natural features have been utilized to serve as primary or secondary security barriers since the beginning of time. When possible, natural barriers should be part of every modern security design.

Manmade physical structural barriers include fences, walls, grills, and bars.

When properly designed and used, both natural and manmade barriers can be attractive and effectively accomplish the following security objectives:

- Define property boundaries
- Deter entry
- Delay and impede unauthorized access
- Direct and restrict the flow of persons and vehicular traffic
- Provide for more efficient and effective deployment of security forces

Perimeter Barriers and Protection

Perimeter protection is the first line of defense against unauthorized access and perhaps the last line of defense against unauthorized egress. The properly designed, installed, and utilized barrier is both a physical and psychological deterrent to unauthorized movement in and out of the facility. An effective barrier deters thefts, intrusions, and vandalism. The perimeter barrier is not a stand-alone or total defense, but must be supplemented with other security assets such as guards, alarms, and CCTV, organizations relying exclusively on physical barriers for their security maybe exposing themselves to crime which may or may not be readily evident. Without additional security measures, some crime such as internal theft, may go on for years without detection.

Walls and fences are the most popular physical barriers and can be constructed out of wood, stone, cement blocks, concrete, and other building materials. Barriers should be constructed in as straight a line as possible to prevent would-be intruders from hiding close to the fence. Obstructions and vegetation should be kept clear or trimmed within 50 feet of either side of the barrier to prevent the hiding of persons, burglary tools or stolen property. Barriers should be examined regularly to check for obstructions and breaks in the barrier and to supplement the effects of the barrier itself. The frequency of patrols depends on the desired degree of security and should always be conducted after extremes in weather or indications of any threat against security.

Fencing

Fencing is generally used to secure larger areas or "Special Security Areas" within an already secured facility. The three most popular types of security fencing are: chain link, barbed wire and concertina wire. The type used depends on the permanence of the fence and the level of security needed.

Chain Link Fencing

Chain link fencing is attractive due to its clean, neat lines. It poses less of a safety hazard because it does not have barbs, yet the small openings still reduce intrusion. Chain link fencing is easily and inexpensively maintained and augmented with the addition of barbed wire and concertina wire.

Barbed Wire Fencing

Except as an addition to the top of chain link fences, barbed wire is rarely used to secure perimeters due to its unsightliness and the danger of inflicting wounds on those who come into contact with it. ..."when barbed wire is used to mark boundaries, it should be five feet high and consist of three to four strands tightly stretched, attached to posts which are from six to ten feet apart". ..."barbed wire on occasion is useful in supplementing natural barriers. For example, barbed wire could be strung along the side of a cliff to further deter intrusions."

Concertina Wire Fencing

Concertina wire is unsightly and hinders ground maintenance, and thus, it should not be used as a permanent barrier without appropriate planning.

Building Security

The second line of defense against unauthorized ingress and egress is the building itself. A perimeter barrier may not always deter the determined intruder. The design of the building and the use of other security measures should be engaged to assist in controlling access and egress. This is especially true where perimeter barriers are located in isolated areas.

Buildings can be intruded from six different directions: the roof (top), flooring/basements (bottom), or one of four sides. Efforts should be made to completely secure the exterior of a structure, but primary consideration is given roof access, doors and entrances, windows and miscellaneous openings such as fire escapes, vents or delivery and trash portals.

One of the most vulnerable sections of any structure is the roof. The roof, especially flat roofs, are difficult to observe, thus affording intruders ample time and concealment to make an entry, and roofs are generally constructed of materials that are easily compromised. When possible, roofs should be constructed of impenetrable materials with a steep pitch, which makes them difficult to maneuver and easy to observe from the ground. ..."the number of attachments to the structure such as fire escapes should be reduced, making it more difficult to obtain access to the roof. Finally, the area immediately surrounding a structure should be kept clear of obstructions so that it would be difficult to hide ladders for example. Reducing access reduces the possibility of illegal entry.

Many unauthorized entries and exits occur through windows. Windows are probably the most vulnerable part of any structure and designing window security for houses of worship can be especially challenging but window security equipment must be considered, especially for windows on the ground level.

Properly installed, the installation of aesthetically appealing metal grates or bars over windows and intrusion detection alarms, many of which are now wireless, will assist in reducing the vulnerability of windows. Proper installation includes tamper resistant connector bolts placed completely through the wall.

Protective windows and window coverings are helpful in deterring the non-professional criminal. With the addition of intrusion detection systems, window protection will also deter the pro. The Uniform Crime Reports consistently point out the large numbers of burglaries and larcenies that are committed by juveniles or nonprofessional criminals.

Doors are also frequently used to obtain illegal access. Many are "soft" and easily violated. Doorways should be well lighted and free from obstructions. Like their counterpart windows, the decorative doors of houses of worship also present unique challenges and security should be a large part of their design and construction. Metal doors are best, and should be equipped, at a minimum, with both deadbolt locks and horizontal retaining bars. When a wooden door is used, the inside should be reinforced to prevent intruders from kicking or cutting a hole through it. Whenever possible, retaining bars with local sounding alarms should be installed on all doors except those most often used.

Special design precautions must be taken when buildings adjoin other structures. When this occurs, it becomes possible to gain entry to a second building by knocking a hole through a common wall. This frequently occurs where a low security structure adjoins a high security structure containing valuables. The entry usually occurs during off-hours, weekends, and holidays when intruders have the time and ability to work unnoticed. When this situation exists security must either be supplemented with alarms, motion detectors, and when possible design and construction correction should be paid to the adjacent facility.

Cooperative Issues

The security posture must be compatible with the daily operations and functions of the facility. Security systems must ensure maximum security while concurrently allowing for normal entries, exits and the conduct of business. To be complete, comprehensive, and effective, the design and installation must be fully integrated as an all-inclusive security, fire, and life-safety system and must be part of an established security plan that includes personnel training and system testing for it to operate properly.

Perimeter security is burdened with the regular comings and goings of employees and visitors and this again presents unique challenges within certain facilities such as houses of worship. It is understandable that high-levels of visible security are likely to be both unattainable and undesirable in select facilities, therefore the administrator and security personnel must consider alternatives such as posting personnel who can visually observe known and welcome persons and look for and react to suspicious behavior while ever mindful that intruders can more easily pass into the facility undetected during the changing of shifts and peak traffic times, unless preventive measures are taken.

When appropriate and feasible, facilities with large numbers of members, employees, contractors, vendors, and visitors may find it necessary or advantageous to issue badges or identification cards. Badges and cards should be color coded for ready identification of personnel and the nature of their presence. Access is then restricted to appropriate areas of the facility. Vendors and contractors, for example, seldom have a legitimate reason to be in certain executive areas. If there is a need for tight security, visitors should be required to make appointments or check-in with a security guard before entering the facility.

Parking areas should enhance the overall security posture of the primary facility and should be located outside the perimeter barrier. This segregation significantly reduces the chances that intruders will successfully enter the facility, when first they must pass a security point on foot. Such an arrangement maximizes access control.

When possible, parking facilities should be located adjacent to the perimeter barrier and guard posts. Parking lots should be well lit to facilitate observation over the facility. Panic alarm stations (blue light stations) should be considered to enable the rapid summons of security personnel. Additionally, the use of CCTV and employment of mobile patrols will complete parking lot security.

It is vital to control the access and egress of employees and visitors and also to control vehicular traffic within the facility. The fewer entrances there are, the easier it is to control the perimeter. Accordingly, only those entrances necessary to the facility should be opened. Perimeter barriers usually have primary entrances and secondary entrances. Utilizing secondary entrances only when absolutely necessary reduces the risk of unauthorized access and the number of personnel needed to secure them. To maximize security, guards should be posted at primary entrances unless they are secured or closed. Secondary entrances should remain secure or locked, and patrolled on a regular basis to guard against intrusion.

Entrance, gate, and transportation dock security is especially important in relation to shipping, receiving and disposal. Security controls, including access and egress, are of vital importance in receiving deliveries and making shipments. Gate security should be utilized for directing facility traffic and serving as a means of checking receivables and shipping. Providing an escort of incoming carriers and vendors at the gate until they reach their destination and when they leave the facility will greatly reduce the opportunity for theft. Personnel should be assigned to monitor the shipping and receiving functions and to compare shipment invoices with loads, either on a continual or random basis, this is especially important to prevent the introduction of hazardous contraband designed to sabotage or otherwise harm the facility.

The disposal of waste and trash provides additional opportunities to secret stolen documents and valuables. Frequently, employees or other persons hide items in trash bins where it is later retrieved. Periodic checks should be made of trash and disposal areas, and vehicles carrying trash should be randomly checked as they leave the facility. Such precautions will reduce thefts and aid in maintaining control over the facility compound. Discarded classified and proprietary information must be destroyed to prevent it from falling into the wrong hands administrators may consider the engagement of a mobile document shredding service for this purpose. Licensed and bonded personnel shred surplus paper documents and computer discs, etc. then provide the client with a certificate of destruction upon completion.

Communication, coordination and cooperation within the organization must be maintained to meet the needs of security. It is important for the security team to monitor the facility's operations so adjustments can be made in security as needs vary and operations change.

People and Hardware

When designing security systems the security professional has a number of alternative protection devices and personnel at his disposal. It is people and hardware that the professional can utilize to supplement the physical barrier. He must analyze the costs, benefits and problems associated with each alternative while choosing those which best meet the specific needs of the facility. No single solution is perfect for every job, and the administrator must take particular care in coordinating with the security professional during this planning stage to analyze organizational needs.

Perimeter barriers maybe supplemented with guard or attendant personnel who boost the deterrent effects of the perimeter barrier and monitor the barrier for defects. The posting of stationary personnel and the use of mobile patrols is largely dependent upon the location and nature of the facility being guarded and the degree of security needed. When perimeter barriers confine an extremely large area, it may be more efficient to utilize mobile guards to observe the total barrier structure. In isolated or semi-isolated areas protection may be reduced to infrequent mobile patrols or only an occasional maintenance check. Heightened security requirements may call for an increase in patrols and/or stationary posts while in some instances adding a second or inner perimeter barrier closer to the area may provide the needed increase in security.

Although reliable as a means of enhancing security, security guards are extremely expensive compared to other physical and electronic security products. The guard force should be reduced to the lowest effective level possible through the use of other security devices such as alarms, clear zones and defensive barriers.

Other Perimeter Barrier Applications

In some facilities – again think museum - it is necessary to construct perimeter barriers around select valuables and historic relics. People by their very nature are curious and may unintentionally damage something while nefarious others may hold evil intentions. Certain applications require special compartmentalized security areas or containers. Other areas may be off-limits due to safety concerns and closed to the public or untrained and unaware employees. Perimeter barriers are also utilized to complement and supplement fire prevention efforts. Security requirements might call for the use of movable barriers which are particularly useful when temporary conditions exist that are especially hazardous or unsafe.

CHAPTER 7

Lighting, Locks, Alarms, and Guards

"At the end of the day, the goals are simple: safety and security" ¬Jodi Rell

Lighting

Protective lighting is deployed to deter unauthorized access and egress from a facility, and when it does not deter, it aids the subsequent detection and apprehension of intruders. The commission of a crime includes three elements: the motive, means, and the opportunity. Effectively deployed, security lighting can reduce or eliminate all three. The placement of security lighting varies depending on need, location, structure, and environment.

Depending on the nature of the facility, protective lighting will be designed to either emphasize the illumination of the perimeter barrier or the interior of the facility. Lighting can be both functional and ornamental (finally some good news for the house of worship). Effective security programs will ensure that the facility is secure at night as well as during the day. Effective lighting enhances the security effort while it serves as a deterrent to criminal activity.

A lighting system must be reliable and designed with overlapping illumination to avoid creating unprotected areas. The design of the exterior security defenses should include lighting in addition to consideration of "panic alarm stations", CCTV, intrusion detection alarms, and electronic access systems.

It is best and most cost-effective to plan for the installation of all exterior electronic protection together. Lighting must provide specified levels of illumination, the following organizations are excellent sources of information relating to security lighting: The *Code of Federal Regulations* lists specific requirements for lighting of protected areas within a perimeter, the *National Parking Association* provides recommendations for the illumination of parking areas, and the *Illinois Engineers Society of North America* provides additional security lighting recommendations.

Safety & Security lighting is used to:

- Prevent crime
- Alleviate fear of crime
- Prevent vehicular and pedestrian traffic accidents
- Promote social interaction
- Promote business and industry
- Contribute to a positive nighttime visual image
- Provide a pleasing daytime appearance
- Provide inspiration for community spirit and growth
- Provide visual information for vehicular and pedestrian traffic
- Facilitate and direct vehicular and pedestrian traffic flow

Planning

Frequently, lighting serves to advertise a product or service during the evening hours, this is problematic when appearance takes precedence to safety and security concerns. The security professional would probably prefer flood lamps mounted near the roof, out of the reach of potential intruders, and directed downward exposing a large area immediately adjacent to the structure.

Conversely, the administrator may prefer floodlights mounted on the ground, illuminating the exterior of the building or a sign for aesthetically pleasing purposes. When protective lighting is used for beautification purposes, it frequently compromises security efforts.

When planning an effective security lighting layout, four factors that must be taken into consideration: brightness, contrast, size, and time. The lighting plan depends on the required level of security and the nature of the objects and environment being secured. Generally, larger, light colored objects require less light than smaller and darker objects. Brightness refers to the reflective ability of the object or structure. Light colors such as white reflect more light than dark colors such as black or brown. Thus, a building painted white would require less light than comparable buildings constructed of dark brick. If there is contrast between the objects being secured and the immediate environment, observation is much easier than if there was little relative contrast. Greater illumination is required for areas that are visually complex or crowded because it is difficult to scan quickly or for extended periods while conversely open spaces require less light because there is more time to observe and focus on foreign objects.

There are three major factors to consider in planning the protective lighting system: security needs, costs, and operational safety. Each safety and security situation must be thoroughly examined with these factors in mind. Only after a complete analysis is made can the best lighting configuration be devised and deployed.

Locks

The physical security of any property or facility starts with its locking system. Locking devices vary greatly in appearance, function, and application.

Regardless of their type, locks are primarily delaying devices. The degree of delay is dependent upon its quality of construction and installation, and the skill of the would-be intruder. The locking device is usually the first line of defense, whether it is on a perimeter fence, a door to the facility, or an interior office.

Locks, like other security hardware vary in quality and application. The administrator and security professional should remain vigilant for violations of key inventories and proper maintenance. A professional licensed and bonded locksmith should be part of the security team.

The types of locks are vast and diverse and the information herein contained only scratches the surface, but it is important that the reader understand that no security system is complete without the employment of the appropriate locks and further that no security plan is complete without the consultation of a locksmith.

Locks provide varying degrees and manners of security. Properly employed, locks will discourage burglars, thieves, or other would-be criminals. To serve as more than delaying devises, locks should be utilized in conjunction with other security hardware as part of the overall security envelope.

Type

- Single Cylinder Locking Devices
- Double Cylinder Locking Devices
- Emergency Exit Locking Devices
- Electromagnetic Locking Devices
- Vertical Throw Devices
- Sequence Locking Devices
- Keying Systems- A key is the standard method of locking and unlocking doors

- Recording Devices- While not a locking device within itself, locks installed in conjunction with an electronic access system will provide a record of door use by time of day and by key used

Most key-operated locks are manufactured to accept a unique key. Locks of any function, quality, or effectiveness, are worthless if keys are not available to those who need them or are not themselves secure and accounted for.

Key Control

A system must be established and enforced that accounts for and controls every key and every lock. Responsibility and authority must be given to someone, preferably within the security department, to maintain records, provide for a key depository, control issuance and retrieval, and investigate any misuse or loss of keys and locks. A written log should be maintained on all keys and locks.

The issuance of keys should be controlled to provide keys only to those persons who have been shown to have a need for keys. When a key is issued, the record should indicate the key number, the name of the person to whom it is assigned, his position within the company, the date of issuance, and any other relevant data. The key log should include records of maintenance and repairs on locks, lost keys and actions taken to remedy any problems detrimental to lock and key security. All keys should be identified and secured in a high-security key cabinet.

Alarms

CAVEAT – Electronic security technology is ever changing and evolving – your security professional must keep abreast of these changes. Alarm companies, manufacturers, vendors, and trade shows offer training and demonstrations of their latest products and peripheral equipment.

Electronic protection of people and property continues to receive great attention. Electronics are utilized to provide perimeter security of a building, doors and windows, access control, control of interior movements, environmental controls, and to detect fire problems. Technology is advancing so rapidly in the area of electronic intrusion detection systems that more and more areas of property are being included in electronic systems. Parking lots, outdoor storage facilities, interior offices, cabinets and safes, and personnel are some areas that are protected with electronics.

Physical security is a matter of degree, with adequate time, equipment, and skills an intruder can penetrate virtually any facility. Intrusion systems must be evaluated in terms of cost-effectiveness. A balance of electronic security features, security personnel, and public law enforcement services should be achieved to provide adequate levels of protection. Over dependence on one component of the system can increase costs beyond benefits, whereas under dependence may result in the degradation of the security system.

All components of a security system must satisfy two practical tests in any organization: 1.The system must function the way it was designed, and 2. be cost-effective for the application. Systems that fail these tests should be redesigned.

Alarm Systems

The functions of the alarm systems:

- Detect fire, intrusion, and environmental concerns
- Make emergency notifications
- Monitor the building, equipment functions, and conditions.

Properly designed systems can incorporate all of the above. Systems can be designed to place emphasis on the priorities of the application, i.e. one facility may have a greater need for intrusion detection than environmental control.

Although many institutions share similar security concerns with other industries, the unauthorized entry of "haters" into targeted facilities is certainly of paramount concern - intrusion detection systems serve to detect, deter, and record unauthorized entry and exit of a facility, building, or other structure.

Alarm systems are installed with the specific needs of the client in mind. The four basic types of alarm signaling systems are defined by their points of termination:

- Central-station alarm systems
- Local alarm systems
- Proprietary central control alarm systems
- Auxiliary alarm systems

The needs of the client usually dictate which of the four basic types of signal termination are most effective and appropriate. In each application, the alarm is sounded and the appropriate response made.

Alarm Stations

Regardless of their termination points, all Alarm Stations monitor fire, intrusion (burglary) environmental and other conditions through the activation of a receiving module at a specific location. Alarm systems function twenty-four hours per day, seven days per week. When an alarm is activated a sensor will notify the intended termination point at the Alarm Station and/or fire or police department.

The response capabilities and requirements of Alarm Stations will be specified within the contract established at the time of purchase, design, and installation and must be set up in the organization's security standard operating procedures. An activated fire sensor requires that the fire department be notified. If the activated sensor is an intrusion alarm, security personnel should be dispatched to the facility and follow their standing operational procedures, generally they should await the arrival of police before entering the facility.

Local Alarms

Local alarm notification systems terminate on-site at either a central control station or in the vicinity of the activated sensor. Local alarms can be visual, audible, or both. Local alarm systems are only effective when someone is present at the facility at all times to monitor the alarms. Without security or monitoring personnel present, local alarm systems do not afford adequate levels of protection. Because they are usually simple in design, unmanned local alarm systems are usually easily defeated, their audible alarms go unanswered and provide little deterrence, and they frequently sound false alarms.

Fundamentals of Alarm Systems

Alarm systems are composed of five basic components:
1. Devices and sensors that monitor and react to a change in the environment
2. Control unit that acts as a signal processing unit
3. Enunciator, either silent or local, that generates human response
4. Power supply from a commercial power source and/or alternative battery power source
5. Circuitry, either hard wire or wireless, for the transmission of signals

These five basic components are common to most alarm systems regardless of their function or purpose. Whether an alarm system is designed for detection of fire, detection of intrusion, emergency notification, or monitoring of equipment or facility conditions, the operating principles of each are much the same.

Selection of Alarm Systems

Each type of alarm detection or notification system is designed to meet the specific needs of the application. The need and feasibility of any alarm system must be determined before installation begins. The following elements should be considered:

- Importance of the facility, materials, and processes
- Vulnerability of the facility, materials, and processes
- Appropriateness and feasibility of using specific types of alarm systems
- Initial and recurring costs of the alarm system compared to the cost of loss of security, valuables, materials, or information
- Savings in manpower and money over a period of time

- Response time by security personnel or other respondents
- Improvement over current security methods

Alarm devices and equipment are classified in three general categories according to the type of physical protection provided; an electronic security system can provide the desired type and depth of protection by combining of two or more of these categories:

- Point or spot protection
- Area or space protection and
- Perimeter protection

Decisions to utilize electronic alarm systems should lead to economy and improvement over existing security practices and methods.

Emergency Notification Systems

Emergency Notification Systems are used to provide warnings during unusual or dangerous situations. Panic/duress alarms and bank robbery notification alarms are perhaps the most common examples of the Emergency Notification Systems. These systems can be designed to provide both local and off-site notification. Strategic placement of devices within a facility one can alert the police or others of an emergency in progress. Robbery alarms should be silent and activated only when safe to do so.

Local audible and visual alarms can be used to notify personnel of an actual or imminent emergency within the facility. When used as part of a comprehensive emergency action plan, whistles, bells, siren, slights and similar devices are effective in warning people to take cover, to evacuate, or to take some other pre-planned action. These systems and devices can be used to warn of an intrusion, fires, explosions, or other man-made or natural disasters.

Monitoring Systems

Electronic Monitoring Systems are generally integrated into the overall electronic security alarm systems and are used to monitor the functions of equipment and machinery for a variety of reasons. Alarms that monitor environmental conditions, temperature and water, for example, are used to protect sophisticated computer equipment from damage or shut-down caused by excessive heat or the introduction of water.

Closed Circuit Television (CCTV) and other electronic surveillance equipment are complimentary additions to monitoring systems. CCTV provides remote overt, discreet, or covert monitoring of a facility and its environment, equipment, personnel, and processes without on-site personnel. CCTV is an effective loss prevention tool and when used in conjunction with a video or digital recorder, CCTV provides a visual record, evidence, of the criminal act and assists in the identification of the perpetrator/s. CCTV systems are frequently used in museums, houses of worship, industrial facilities, retail stores, hospitals, hotels, banks, office buildings, and other areas.

The basic components of a CCTV system consist of a camera, a monitor, connecting circuitry, and a power source. Expanded systems with numerous cameras, monitors, recorders, remote control, and other features are often cost effective when considering the reduction in security personnel required and the resultant security advantage afforded and is likely to be much more cost effective than other systems depending on needs and application.

Access Control Systems

Controlling access and egress from facilities is a primary function of all security systems. Access control, as defined here, is an electronic means of controlling and monitoring the movement of people or vehicles in and out of secured areas.

Electronic Access Control Systems identify and record who passed through a protected area and when. These systems are computerized and provide immediate information on; who gains access to the facility, where and when.

Access control systems are programmed to allow or disallow access to restricted places based on a number of criteria such as; time, personnel, day of week, and frequency of access. The system operates by a person introducing either coded access cards, push button (combination) sequences, or a combination of both. The latest technology includes biometric sensors that verify fingerprints, handprints, eye images or voice patterns and are used where the highest levels of security are required.

When integrated with intrusion alarm systems, access points can generate alarm signals when doors or gates have been compromised by force, or have been propped open or left ajar.

Guards

With the Physical Security systems in place it is time to incorporate the specialist who is going to deter crime and criminality by his physical presence and who is going to monitor those systems and respond to the alarms.

Private security personnel now outnumber public law enforcement officers in the United States. Overburdened public law enforcement cannot and frequently will not provide security services to private enterprise – therefore it is imperative that administrators and their security personnel develop effective lines of communication with their police agencies based on dignity and mutual respect.

Growing crime rates and a public perception of out-of-control crime exacerbated by the horrific headlines generated by Hate-Crimes has established the need for extensive private security services in the private sector. A facility or organization that does not project a perception of security and wellbeing does not have adequate security.

Security is as much a perception as it is a reality, members and employees who feel vulnerable and insecure will be every bit as restless and non-productive as those who actually don't have security in their meeting-places, house of worship, or workplace.

Security Guard Duties

This is a rather complex issue, due to the wide variety of duties and functions performed by employees in the broad category of Private Security Personnel.

In addressing this issue, the Private Security Task Force emphasized the need for job descriptions for private security personnel. The task found,..."as a general guide, the data recorded in job descriptions should relate to two essential features of each position: 1. the nature of the work involved, and 2. the employee type who appears best fitted for the position."

Guard and patrol services include the provision of personnel who perform the following functions, either contractually or internally, at such places and facilities as religious and charitable institutions, libraries and museums, industrial plants, financial institutions, educational institutions, office buildings, retail establishments, commercial complexes, hotels and motels, health care facilities, recreation facilities, residences, housing developments, transportation vehicles and facilities and others:

- Prevention and/or detection of intrusion, unauthorized entry or activity, vandalism, or trespass on private property
- Prevention and/or detection of theft, loss, embezzlement, misappropriation or concealment of merchandise, money, bonds, stocks, notes, or other valuable documents or papers
- Control, regulation, or direction of the flow or movements of the public, whether by vehicle or otherwise, to assure the protection of property;
- Protection of individuals from bodily harm
- Enforcement of rules, regulations, and policies related to crime reduction

These functions may be provided at single or multiple locations. Guard functions are generally provided at one central location for one client or employer. Patrol functions, however, are performed at several locations, often for several clients.

Summary

The administrator and security professional should have an understanding of the effective and efficient usage, applications, operations, and principles of Physical Security Systems and Guard Services. They also must be aware that all systems have weak points by which their functioning can be minimized, disrupted, or by-passed - yet most will prove satisfactory if properly selected, installed, and maintained.

Electronic access, warning, CCTV, and detection systems are extremely beneficial in a wide variety of applications; however, administrators and security personnel should plan each application carefully and thoroughly analyze their security needs and the systems available before making a decision and once engaged they must include training on these systems in their security plans.

CHAPTER 8

"Better be despised for too anxious apprehensions, than ruined by too confident security" -Edmund Burke

Just envision the moment you realize that your computer was hacked and that your organization's membership list has been posted on the internet and that your business records have been compromised – now you see the need for information security.

The final line of defense at any facility is the high security storage area. The nature of the business being conducted, the levels of desired security, and the items or valuables being protected will dictate the level of security for any facility. Every facility has unique security requirements. The following are general principles, which apply to all security programs.

The type and quality of security storage containers will depend on what is being protected. A security storage container for classified documents will be different from one for jewels or precious metals. Fire resistant containers are more appropriate for paper documents, whereas a tamper-proof, burglary-resistant unit would be required for the jewels or precious metals.

Security storage containers are generally either fire resistant or burglary resistant but not always both. New advances in technology are addressing this and many of the newer state-of-the-art security containers will provide a greater measure of protection against both fire and theft. However, most storage containers usually only serve one specialized function and provide only minimum protection in the other area. Costs can be greatly reduced by purchasing a container that will serve only one function and provide only one type of protection.

Safes

Because they are usually very expensive, careful attention must be given to the particular needs and application before selecting a safe.

Safes are designated alphabetically in two categories to describe the degree of protection they provide:

- Fire resistive
- Burglary and robbery resistive

The fire protection rating of safes is established by the Safe Manufacturers National Association and independent tests conducted by Underwriter's Laboratories (UL).

No safe is totally safe! The old axiom "you get what you pay for" certainly applies to safes. The burglary resistant properties provided by a safe are in direct proportion to its quality and cost.

Additional measures should be taken to enhance a safe's protective qualities. Perimeter barriers, adequate locking hardware, electronic alarm systems, or other security procedures must be employed to achieve the highest levels of security. How a safe is used is just as important as its quality. Safes should not be placed in remote, poorly lit locations within the facility. Rather, the safe should be placed where unauthorized access is likely to be discovered. Combinations and key inventory control must be strictly secured. As with other locking devises, the combinations and keys should be expertly changed regularly.

The security of a safe can frequently and easily be improved by taking simple steps to reduce its vulnerability. Industry standards dictate that all safes weighing less than 750 pounds be anchored to the building structure, thus making its removal from the premises more difficult. For example, this is quite common when a fire resistant safe is purchased and is encased in concrete. This increases its fire resistant qualities and also makes it less vulnerable to other safecracking techniques and removal.

Vaults

A vault is a room designed for the secure storage of valuables and is different from a safe in that it is larger, a part of the building structure, and is constructed of different materials and is designed to accommodate entry by one or more people. Ratings for vaults are established by the Insurance Services Office and are based on the type of construction materials utilized, their relative thickness, construction standards, and equipment features. Construction standards and equipment features must be met in certain rating categories, such as inclusion of combination locks and time locks.

Electronic alarm protection and electronic access systems provide a greater measure of security and accountability. The use of an electronic access system in addition to the combination locks provides an audit trail of persons using the vault and access is easily denied pending establishment of a new combination when needed. Additional protection of the vault can be provided by area or space devices such as motion detectors which react to anyone moving into the area around the vault, CCTV, and other electronic security applications.

When constructing vaults and other high security "safe rooms" within an already secured facility, requirements outlined in Department of Defense (DOD) and Director, Central Intelligence (DCI) specifications can provide invaluable assistance.

Information Security

The security of records and information is absolutely vital to the effective continued operation of all organizations. The loss or destruction of such information or compromise of its confidentiality will likely result in one or more of the following:

- Interrupted operational capability
- Loss of confidential information
- Inability to provide services
- Inability to satisfy certain legal requirements or contractual obligations
- Damaged dealings with suppliers
- Financial harm to the organization

The need to protect proprietary information is absolute!

Proprietary information comes in a variety of forms and its relative importance varies from organization to organization. The first step in providing security and protection of information is to develop a procedure for the evaluation and control of information. At a minimum, the following steps must be taken in establishing an information protection program:

- An ongoing inventory of all records, documents, and information
- The objective appraisal of the organizational value of the information, records, or documents
- Development of an information security classification system

- Employ appropriate levels of security as determined by the information classification system

When the sources and types of information have been identified, a classification system must be developed to differentiate between vital and non-vital records. Different terms can be used to separate and identify the various categories of information according to organizational value. One common example of classification is the following:

- Vital Records are essentially irreplaceable and are of the greatest value to the continued operation of the organization.
- Important Records can only be replaced with great expense and inconvenience
- Useful Records are records which when lost would create inconveniences but could be replaced rather quickly and inexpensively
- Nonessential Records are unessential to effective organizational operation

Protective measures

The protection of information is accomplished by; procedural controls, duplication, and storage.

Procedural control applies to all aspects of security and especially so in information security. The process of information classification is the first step in controlling the flow of information through the organization.

Controls must be established that limits the availability, responsibility, and accountability of information to personnel and restricted or based only on "the need to know and the right to know". Organizational records must be secured and protected in descending order of importance, the more vital the record or information, the higher the level of control and security.

Duplication of records is both a security risk and a security asset. It serves as a "backup" to records that can be lost, stolen, or destroyed. It also provides the same information as the originals, thus requiring the same level of security as the originals. When copying documents and records care must be exercised to prevent unauthorized duplication and the subsequent dissemination outside the organization. Duplicated vital records should be secured off-site to avoid loss to natural and manmade threats so if the source of information is lost, the organization can continue without interruption, licensed and bonded classified material storage companies offer these services.

Computer Security

Computer Security begins with security of the hardware and extends to include the storage of information. The loss of a laptop for example, is the loss of expensive hardware as well as the proprietary information contained therein.

Computer and information theft has become commonplace, therefore, strict accountability in the issuance of computers and requirements to utilize physical security measures to guard against hardware theft is critical.

Computers have greatly increased the ability to store, retrieve, manipulate, and transmit vital information. Accordingly, computers have become targets of theft. The misuse, damage, or loss of a computer can render helpless or irreparably damage an entire organization. Electronic data processing systems must be afforded a high level of security.

Access to, and operation of, computer units must be strictly controlled. Attempts to enter, manipulate or otherwise obtain information must be preventable and detectable.

Storage of data and programs on magnetic tapes, cards, discs, or drums is a vital part of any computer security operation. Steps must be taken to provide security for the physical storage of tapes, cards, discs, etc. As with "paper" records, duplicated records should be secured off-site. In addition to electronic "cloud sites" special storage units for the various data forms are available which provide not only security but also a controlled environment. Excessive heat and humidity in a storage unit or tape library can damage or destroy electronic information. Electronic access and alarm systems can monitor and alarm "water & high temp" allowing for repairs to environmental control systems before damage occurs. Risks involving computers include water, fire, espionage, sabotage, accidental losses, theft, fraud, embezzlement and natural disasters.

Summary

The security requirements of each facility must be established by considering and evaluating needs based on; physical factors, type and extent or risk exposure, and business conducted. The effectiveness of a security program; safe, vault, or other, is in direct proportion to the depth of security that decreases the chances for criminal success. Information is a critical asset and must be protected accordingly. An in-depth evaluation of all records is mandatory in determining the appropriate level of security for the control of the flow and storage of information, records, and documents – paper and electronic.

*"Historically, privacy was almost implicit, because it was hard to find and gather information. But in the digital world, whether it's digital cameras or satellites or just what you click on, we need to have more explicit rules - not just for governments but for private companies." –*Bill Gates

"...the wolly theme of being safe everywhere" –Winston Churchill

The leadership of every organization has a responsibility to develop and implement programs in safety and fire prevention with the goals of protecting life and property, and to prevent, reduce, or eliminate loss. Fire is a major threat to life and property in any business, and administrators and security personnel should be aware of the fundamentals of fire and fire protection. As with police departments, administrators and security personnel would be well-advised to establish a good working relationship within their fire department, develop a line of communication, and avail themselves of the fire prevention, safety, and training programs they offer.

Fire Protection

"Don't let your dreams go up in smoke" -Anonymous

Security may have either a direct or indirect organizational responsibility for the development, operation, and enforcement of a fire safety program. Established security programs assist in fire safety by; facilitating and controlling the movement of persons in the facility, ensuring orderly conduct on the property, and protecting life and property at all times. Security operations should provide the following in support of the fire safety program:

Security's Role

- Prevent unauthorized access to persons who might set a fire

- Control the activities of people authorized to be on the property and assist anyone who may not be aware of fire safety policies
- Control pedestrian and vehicular traffic during fire drills and evacuation during actual emergencies
- Control of roads, gates, driveways and vehicular traffic to facilitate access by the fire and police departments
- Checking conditions of "hot work", including cutting and welding, and if necessary, prepare to operate fire extinguishing equipment
- Practice diligence in observing conditions likely to cause a fire
- Routine examinations of firefighting equipment; extinguishers, sprinkler systems, etc.
- Performing tests of firefighting equipment and conducting fire drills.
- Operating fire control equipment after sounding the alarm and before the response of others persons to the fire
- Monitoring signals fire alarm and detection systems
- Ensuring patrol routes provide surveillance of potential fire hazards

Security Guard Post Orders should include:

- Ensure that doors, gates, windows, skylights, fire doors, and fire shutters are closed and locked properly
- Ensure the removal or proper storage of combustible materials
- Ensure that all fire apparatus is in place and accessible
- Ensure that exits and aisles are clear and exit signs are properly posted and functional
- Secure machinery carelessly left running
- Checking the facility for carelessly discarded smoking materials

- Check space heaters
- Ensure that hazardous manufacturing and operating procedures are maintained in a safe condition
- Check sprinkler valve pressure gauges
- Check for proper operation of heating, ventilation and air conditioning equipment (HVAC)
- Close leaking air and water valves
- Carefully patrol areas of renovation and new construction – be alert to fire and safety threats
- Record and report violations of safety & security policies – ensure repairs to dangerous situations

Training for Fire Prevention and Protection

Administrators and security personnel must be thoroughly acquainted with the property they are protecting and the policies, procedures, and programs implemented to guide them in their duties. All personnel must be familiar with the physical features of the property including fire exits, the materials utilized and stored on the premises, and the fire suppression and detection equipment, and materials, their location, and proper operation. Proper training for security personnel should include the classes of fire, basic first aid, extinguishing agents and equipment, and available support services.

Classes of Fire

The four classes of fire:

1. Class A – Common combustibles; wood, paper, cloth, rubber, and some plastics
2. Class B – Flammable liquids; petroleum-based gas, and oil products, etc.
3. Class C – Electrical equipment
4. Class D – Combustible metals; sodium, magnesium, and potassium, etc.

The class of a fire is defined by its type of fuel. To properly and effectively suppress a fire, it is important to accurately define its fuel source. A basic knowledge of the combustibles is needed to select the proper extinguishing agent.

Extinguishers

Fire extinguishers are designed to discharge a specific type of fire extinguishing agent. Effectiveness depends on using the proper extinguisher and extinguishing agent for the fire encountered. Some extinguishers are effective on only one type of fire, while others are suitable for two or more classes of fire. Fire Extinguishers are classified as A, B, C or D according to the class of fire they are designed to extinguish and selecting the proper extinguisher depends primarily on the hazards present at a particular facility, generally a "mix" of types is appropriate. Extinguishers must be properly located and maintained.

Security and safety departments should ensure that those responsible properly maintain all fire suppression equipment. Before deciding which extinguishers to purchase and where to place them, an in-depth survey of the facility must be made – this is the perfect time to request the assistance for your fire department, defer to them as they are the experts. After extinguishers are selected, security personnel and other employees must be properly trained in their use. Fire Departments, Zoning and Building Departments, Fire Marshals, and OSHA are excellent sources of additional information on industrial fire safety.

Sprinkler Protection

Portable fire extinguishers are transported to a fire location. Fixed or stationary fire extinguishing equipment is designed to control and extinguish a fire in a specific area. Fixed fire extinguishing systems utilize a variety of extinguishing agents – from water to chemical agents, depending on the application. They are automatic and discharge the extinguishing agent upon activation and many are integrated into the electronic alarm system.

Fire Protection Signals

Protective signaling devices play a major role in fire detection and protection and are used to:
- Notify people of a fire
- Call or alert the fire department and other professionals
- Monitor extinguishing systems and warn of activation, tampering and malfunctions
- Monitor industrial processes and warn of hazardous conditions
- Activate control and suppression equipment

The very early stages of a fire are critical in detection, protection, containment, and suppression thus making signaling devices an invaluable part of any fire safety and integrated security system. Early detection can literally mean the difference between life and death. The presence and proper functioning of a protective signaling system is a major element in all safety and security programs. As in all electronic safety and security equipment, fire alarm and detection technology changes frequently.

Workplace Fire Safety

The National Fire Safety Council and the National Fire Protection Association report that fire losses exceed more than $2.2 billion annually and more than 5000 people are killed each year in fires in the United States. These organizations along with the U.S. Department of Labor, Occupational Safety and Health Administration (OSHA) set standards and provide literature pertaining to workplace fire safety.

Workplace Safety

Federal, state and local laws and the standards set by insurance carriers require employers to provide a safe and healthful work environment for employees. Again, OSHA is an excellent source of materials relating to workplace safety. Some jurisdictions have work-safety regulations, and environmental protection laws, that are more stringent than those established by OSHA and the federal government and insurance companies may set additional standards.

Accident Prevention

An effective accident prevention and occupational safety program in the work place is a prime part of the security and safety operation. All employees must be initially trained and periodically retrained in general safety practices and in specific job related responsibilities. Safety awareness, from the top of the management hierarchy to the lowest job classification, is imperative if safety hazards and violations are to be found, understood, and eliminated.

The security plan must play a major role in safety and accident prevention. Administrators and security personnel should be trained and knowledgeable of required safety standards and practices. The security professional is responsible for correcting or bringing about the correction of safety hazards and violations. Routine security duties; patrols, inspections, access control, etc., expose security personnel to most if not all of the work environment, employees, and operations and potential safety problems and violations.

Summary

Fire is one of the most destructive forces known to man and can occur as an act of nature, as an accident, or as an act of sabotage – arson. Regardless of its source, the potential for its occurrence can be reduced and resulting damage limited, with an adequate fire prevention, protection, and suppression program. Training and practice, along with a basic knowledge of fire characteristics, and fire suppression techniques and equipment can greatly reduce the fire threat.

AFTERWORD

You cannot serve and protect others unless you adequately protect yourself – the organization must possess a robust safety and security program that by its very nature provides that organization with the teams, tools, and techniques needed to serve others.

Going forward remember the root-cause of the threat but don't be blinded by it, keep in mind the old adage; "can't see the forest because of the trees" – the safety and security of your organization and its most important resource, people, is a comprehensive goal that should not be limited to a single or immediate threat but rather must encompass the broad spectrum of threats and hazards, manmade and natural.

Please utilize the many resources cited throughout this work and those listed within the Resources and Acknowledgements section that follows. I urge you to avail yourselves of the valuable assistance they render, develop in-depth and meaningful relationships with your police agencies and fire departments, become members of groups within the broad coalition of those organizations and groups dedicated to eradicating crime and take professional and proactive measures to protect and serve.

It is my sincere hope that I have provided the reader with usable information and that I have inspired you to help protect those unable to protect themselves,

Charlie

RESOURCES, ACKNOWLEDGEMENTS, and CREDITS

When you need help get it from the experts!

Material for this book was assembled from many sources including the persons, agencies, organizations, and public domain sources listed below, this work would not have been possible without them, I applaud their professional approach to public safety and I encourage the readers to avail themselves of these expert resources:

American Society of Industrial Security
Aspen Risk Management Group
Law Enforcement Assistance Administration
National Locksmith Association
National Burglar and Fire Alarm Association
International Association of Chiefs of Police
Lion Investigation Academy
Underwriters Laboratories
Insurance Service Office
Safe Manufacturers National Association
National Bureau of Standards
National Fence Association
National Fire Protection Association
National Fire Safety Council
Occupational Safety and Health Administration
Federal Emergency Management Agency
Federal Bureau of Investigation
Department of Justice
Benjamin B. Wagner, U.S. Attorney, E/CA
Department of State
Department of Homeland Security
Director, Central Intelligence
U.S. Air Force, U.S. Army, U.S. Coast Guard
U.S. Marine Corps and U.S. Navy
American Society of Criminology
The Anti-Defamation League
The Department of Homeland Security
CA Office of Emergency Services

Advising Houses of Worship on a Comprehensive and Balanced Security Plan, by Chief William Carcara, International Association of Chiefs of Police

Houses of Worship Security Practices Guide, Department of Homeland Security

Guide for Developing High - Quality Emergency Operations Plans for Houses of Worship, FEMA

Hate Crime, information and resources regarding hate crimes and bias available on line at: National Crime Prevention Council

House of Worship Security Self-Assessment, is offered free of charge by the American Crime Prevention Institute and security giant Honeywell

Principles of Security Consulting, by Charles Read

MAXIMUM SECURITY...Defusing the Threat... by Major Charles Read

ABOUT THE AUTHOR

Mr. Read served concurrently in Public Safety and the Military for over twenty years. His specialties within the NY State Police and PA Office of Attorney General included Organized Crime, Major Frauds, Financial Crimes, Official Misconduct, Criminal Intelligence, and Dignitary Protection. His military accomplishments include service as a Coast Guard Intelligence and Logistics Officer (counter-terrorism) at the 1984 Summer Olympic Games and as a Chief of Security Police within the elite Air Force Special Operations Command where he directed missions in the United States, England, Honduras, Korea, Japan, Puerto Rico, and Saudi Arabia.

Mr. Read served as Town Manager - Chief Executive Officer - of an upscale municipality where he exercised command authority over all town departments, personnel, programs, and functions.

CREDENTIALS
- Certified Security Consultant
- Certified Fraud Consultant
- Licensed Firearms Instructor
- Certified Arbitrator – BBB
- Certified NIMS Instructor - FEMA
- Licensed Private Investigator

CONSULTANCIES
- PricewaterhouseCoopers
- Lloyds of London
- Loomis-Fargo
- FELD Entertainment
- Police Dept. Sea Gate NY
- Ringling Brothers Circus
- CB Richard Ellis

"Only a life lived for others is a life worthwhile." – Albert Einstein